WELCOME

General Norman Schwarzkopf led the Coalition forces that ejected the Iraqis from Kuwait in Operation Desert Storm. *(US Department of Defense via Wikimedia Commons)*

WAR AND RUINOUS war…The Ba'athist regime of Iraq and its ruthless leader Saddam Hussein had brought death and economic hardship to their people. The ruling Sunni minority in the country managed to maintain a stranglehold on power, suppressing dissent within through secret police, kidnapping, summary executions, and terrorising their own population, even using poison gas.

At the same time, Saddam provoked a war with neighbouring Iran, invading that country and spawning an eight-year conflict that brought only more death and misery, ending much as it had begun – except for those who had perished in the conflagration. Then, with bluster and threat, the Iraqi strongman perpetrated yet another act of aggression. On August 2, 1990, his army, a still formidable force, surged across the frontier with Kuwait and seized the country in a frenzy of armed aggression, cruelty, and outright crimes against humanity.

Saddam's reasons for the invasion of Kuwait were notable – to distract the Iraqi people from their domestic troubles and economic woes, to seize the oil production capacity and wealth of Kuwait that he had watched with a jealous eye for many years, and to assert Iraqi primacy among Arab nations and across the Middle East. And then, there was more. Without question, Saddam Hussein sought to satiate his own thirst for power in an exercise of aggrandisement. No matter how much another military adventure might cost, his delusions of intoxicating power drove him to military aggression once again.

But in his twisted strategy to achieve Iraqi hegemony in the region, there was one colossal miscalculation. Saddam and his cadre of sycophant diplomats and generals failed in their assessment of the worldwide response to the horrific invasion and seven-month occupation of Kuwait. As reports of the Iraqi rape and pillage of Kuwait surfaced, the civilized world recoiled and then galvanized behind the leadership of President George HW Bush, Prime Ministers Margaret Thatcher and John Major, and the governments of Arab countries, such as Saudi Arabia, Qatar, Bahrain, and Syria, which saw the Iraqi aggression as a threat to their own security. Depending on the source and the nature of contribution, at least 35 and as many as 42 countries joined the Coalition that soon took the necessary action.

For Saddam Hussein, the notion that his armed forces could withstand the mighty buildup of Operation Desert Shield and the unleashing of retribution in Desert Storm, seems unimaginable to reasonable people, both experts in international dynamics and common individuals. Defeat was inevitable, and the vaunted Iraqi army was devastated as the "Mother of all Battles" became a colossal embarrassment for Saddam on the global stage. And yet, he remained in power, a survivor amid utter defeat.

The politics of war and the price of stability rather than chaos in the Middle East weighed heavily on the decision to halt offensive operations against Iraq. That decision is still debated today. This volume explores the political, diplomatic, strategic and tactical convergence that led to the greatest military endeavour since World War Two. Welcome to Desert Storm 35.

Michael E Haskew
Editor

Saddam Hussein exudes power and confidence for the Iraqi press.
(Iraqi News Agency via Wikimedia Commons)

Soldiers of the Coalition, these US troops pose with a Stinger portable missile launcher.
(US Air Force via Wikimedia Commons)

CONTENTS

The blackened hulk of an Iraqi T-72 main battle tank lies abandoned in the desert after the onslaught of Coalition forces in the Gulf War. *(US Government via Wikimedia Commons)*

Many nations came together to form the Coalition that won the victory over Iraqi military aggression against Kuwait in the 1991 Gulf War. *(US Government via Wikimedia Commons)*

General Norman Schwarzkopf addresses troops during Operation Desert Shield. *(US Department of Defense via Wikimedia Commons)*

A Royal Air Force Panavia Tornado attack aircraft sits beneath a shelter at a Saudi air base. *(US Army Center for Military History via Wikimedia Commons)*

Soldiers of the British 1st Armoured Division dig their trapped vehicle out of the desert sand in January 1991. *(US Army via Wikimedia Commons)*

Shown in company with escort and support ships, the aircraft carrier USS *Independence* and her strike group were among the first forces deployed to the Persian Gulf. *(US Navy via Wikimedia Commons)*

Main cover image:
A US tank battalion on the move during Operation Desert Shield, 1991. *(Peter Turnley/ Corbis/VCG via Getty Images)*

ISBN: 978 1 83632 225 2
Editor: Mike Haskew
Senior editor, specials: Roger Mortimer
Email: roger.mortimer@keypublishing.com
Cover Design: Steve Donovan
Design: SJmagic DESIGN SERVICES, India
Advertising Sales Manager: Sam Clark
Email: sam.clark@keypublishing.com
Tel: 01780 755131
Advertising Production: Becky Antoniades
Email: Rebecca.antoniades@keypublishing.com

SUBSCRIPTION/MAIL ORDER
Key Publishing Ltd, PO Box 300,
Stamford, Lincs PE9 1NA
Tel: 01780 480404
Subscriptions email: subs@keypublishing.com
Mail Order email: orders@keypublishing.com
Website: www.keypublishing.com/shop

PUBLISHING
Group CEO: Adrian Cox
Publisher: Steve O'Hara

Published by
Key Publishing Ltd, PO Box 100,
Stamford, Lincs PE9 1XQ
Tel: 01780 755131
Website: www.keypublishing.com

PRINTING
Precision Colour Printing Ltd, Haldane,
Halesfield 1, Telford, Shropshire
TF7 4QQ

DISTRIBUTION
Frontline Distribution Solutions Ltd,
2 Poultry Avenue, London, EC1A 9PU
Enquiries: 02074 294000 or info@flgroup.co.uk

KEY Publishing

SEEDS OF CONFLICT

SADDAM HUSSEIN WAS belligerent and brutal, willing to sacrifice his own people in the crucible of war or in crushing domestic opposition. Within months of his rise to complete power in Iraq, he launched an invasion of Iran that resulted in a disastrous eight-year conflagration.

The Iraqi invasion of Iran came on the heels of accusations hurled at the Islamic Republic, and its leader Ayatollah Khomeini, in an effort to justify military action. Saddam Hussein accused the Iranians of supporting the Shi'ite Muslim majority in Iraq to oppose his Ba'ath Party rule. While asserting that the Iranians had not only fomented unrest in his country, but also encouraged terrorism within, Saddam further eyed control of the vital Shatt al Arab waterway.

The confluence of the fabled Tigris and Euphrates rivers in the "cradle of civilisation", the Shatt al Arab courses 120 miles to its terminus with the Persian Gulf. The waterway forms a boundary between Iraq and Iran while serving as Iraq's only direct access to the Gulf. Complete control of the waterway would provide Saddam Hussein with substantial leverage in the oil-rich Middle East and beyond with greater influence on the economic stability of the West.

The result of Saddam's invasion of Iran, however, was a costly war that ended in stalemate. The course of the conflict left Iraq with an estimated 300,000 dead and 900,000 wounded, while Iran suffered even more with 400,000 killed and approximately 1,000,000 wounded. Amazingly, in comparison to the populations of the two countries, these casualties were the highest of any conflict in the 20th century. In addition to the horrific battle casualties his military sustained, Saddam had taken the opportunity to use chemical weapons against his own people, particularly those Shi'ite and Kurdish factions that he considered a direct domestic threat.

The end of the 1980-88 war left Iraq in tremendous debt. Saddam had borrowed heavily from both Saudi Arabia and Kuwait.

Sadam Hussein meets the president of the Yemen Arab Republic, Ali Abdullah Saleh, in June 1990. *(Public Domain Government of Yemen via Wikimedia Commons)*

While the cost of the war has been estimated at $600bn, in a pragmatic gesture with designs on another military campaign, the government of Iraq relinquished its minor territorial gains to the Iranians in the hopes of securing their neutrality in his coming aggression against Kuwait. At the same time, Saddam evaluated his situation comprehensively. Although the war had ended badly, he maintained a battle-hardened army of more than half a million troops along with Soviet-made tanks and armoured vehicles, as well as substantial artillery.

Saddam's focus on Kuwait sharpened in the late 1980s for several reasons. Traditionally, Iraq had claimed that Kuwait was actually a part of its own Basra province and had been recognised as such by the Ottoman Empire. In the early 1920s, the British had drawn the boundary between Iraq and Kuwait with little regard for historical precedent or future conflict. The international boundary left Iraq virtually landlocked, while the Kuwaitis turned a deaf ear to overtures for territorial concessions later.

For decades, Kuwait had been under British rule, but in 1961 the nation was granted its independence. From there came a renewed wave of Iraqi pressure and soon enough sabre rattling was underway. Saddam asserted the old Iraqi claim on Kuwaiti territory and threw in additional charges for public consumption. First, he said that Kuwait had intentionally depressed the global price of oil, substantially exceeding the production limits established by the Organization of Petroleum Exporting Countries (OPEC). Further, he made a forceful demand that Kuwait and Saudi Arabia erase the massive debt that Iraq had incurred with them during the war with Iran.

American Ambassador to Iraq April Glaspie meets Saddam Hussein in Baghdad, July 1990. *(Public Domain Imad marie via Wikimedia Commons)*

Amid rising tensions in the Middle East, Saddam Hussein and King Hussein of Jordan held talks in February 1990. *(Public Domain Government of Iraq via Wikimedia Commons)*

Striking a pose with other Arab leaders, including King Hussein of Jordan and Hosni Mubarak of Egypt, Saddam Hussein smiles during a ride in an open-topped limousine. *(Public Domain Government of Iraq via Wikimedia Commons)*

April Glaspie, US Ambassador to Iraq, held a pivotal meeting with Saddam Hussein in July 1990. *(US Government via Wikimedia Commons)*

and the United Arab Emirates of collusion in the ongoing slump in oil prices. The Kuwaitis, Saddam said, were also stealing Iraqi oil through a process of slant drilling in the vast Rumaila oil field in southern Iraq, roughly 30 miles west of the port city of Basra.

The stakes in the burgeoning conflict between Iraq and Kuwait were raised considerably when the geopolitical and economic influence of Saudi Arabia was brought into the equation. The oil-derived wealth of the Saudis and the Western dependence on their oil exports were apparent to the rest of the world. For Saddam Hussein, control of not only Iraqi oil production and distribution, but also that of Kuwait, and perhaps even Saudi Arabia, was a tantalising prospect. He considered the eminent position that Iraq would achieve throughout the Middle East and his own compelling role in global affairs should his ambitions be realised.

Contemplating such an outcome with diplomatic intimidation and the threat of force as his levers, Saddam envisioned the power associated with control of roughly 20%

Together, the Ba'athist regime owed its financiers in Saudi Arabia and Kuwait an estimated total of $37bn, and $14bn of that belonged to the Kuwaitis. When Saddam's demand was rejected, he was incensed and further determined to exploit a perceived opportunity to bully or even occupy his Arab neighbour to the south. For good measure, the Iraqis added to their list of grievances against Kuwait. They demanded a lease of the islands of Bubiyan and Warbah, which were located in the path of Iraqi access to the Persian Gulf, and accused the Kuwaitis

Emir of Kuwait Jaber Al-Ahmad Al-Sabah met with President George HW Bush at The White House in 1990. *(US Government via Wikimedia Commons)*

Control of the Shatt al Arab waterway was a key objective of Saddam Hussein during the Iran-Iraq War. *(Public Domain Aziz1005 via Wikimedia Commons)*

of the world's estimated 102 trillion barrels of crude oil reserves. Already, Iraq held 100 billion barrels, Kuwait 97 billion, the United Arab Emirates 98 billion, and Saudi Arabia a massive 257 billion barrels. Further, a Middle Eastern power play with a potent military force at his disposal would distract the Iraqi people from their losses in lives, treasure, and economic hardships that had resulted from the war with Iran, erase the debt to Kuwait, while probably convincing the Saudis to cancel their own credit repayment, and essentially pave the way for Iraqi hegemony in the region, supplanting Egypt and Saudi Arabia in the role.

In the late 1980s, there were some temporary improvements in relations between Iraq and Saudi Arabia and Kuwait, with non-aggression pacts and agreements for Kuwait to supply water for human consumption and irrigation to Iraq. However, an agreement for the Kuwaitis to lease Bubiyan and Warbah, allowing better access from the Iraqi port of Umm Qasr to the sea, remained a thorny issue. At the same time, relations between Iraq and the rest of the Arab world deteriorated due to violence and repression of foreign residents within Saddam's domain. Human rights violations were noted, but little was done

in response. Statements of condemnation rang hollow in Saddam's ears, no doubt emboldening his future course of action.

The Iraqi strongman steadily grew more bellicose, threatening the use of chemical weapons against Israel should that nation exercise military force against his country. The statement referenced the Israeli air strike of June 7, 1981, dubbed Operation Opera, that crippled a major Iraqi nuclear facility at Osirak near Baghdad. Then, by the summer of 1990, Saddam was publicly threatening military activity to redress Iraqi grievances against Kuwait. By extension, the security of Saudi Arabia was also on the table.

The American response to Iraqi provocations included a heightened status of alert for elements of the US Navy's Seventh Fleet, headquartered in Yokosuka, Japan, that had been deployed to the Arabian Sea and other Middle Eastern waters. Intelligence reports delivered alarming news that Iraq had moved at least 30,000 troops and accompanying armour to the frontier with Kuwait. By July, Saddam Hussein had become convinced that other Arab nations were engaged in a joint effort to oppose his developing campaign of intimidation. While Kuwait appeared to be strengthening ties with Syria and Egypt, he also took note of Kuwaiti diplomatic overtures with Iran, ethnically Persian, and his most recent military adversary.

At a meeting of the Arab League in Baghdad in May 1990, Saddam had already attempted to assert Iraqi leadership in the region with a denunciation of Israel and a consolidated stance against the Jewish state and its Western supporters, particularly the United States. At the same time, he laid out his complaints against Kuwait. According to the *New York Times*, he told the other leaders present: "The policies of some Arab rulers are American… They are inspired by America to undermine Arab interests and security." These remarks

This Iraqi T-62 tank was destroyed in battle in Iran during the war of 1980-88. *(Creative Commons Hamed Saber via Wikimedia Commons)*

A large contingent of Iraqi soldiers surrenders to Iranian forces in Khorramshahr. *(GNU Free Documentation License Sajed.ir via Wikimedia Commons)*

The port of Basra remains a centre of the Iraqi oil export trade. *(Creative Commons Aziz1005 via Wikimedia Commons)*

of Kuwait and the United Arab Emirates as tantamount to military action against Iraq. In that case, she concluded: "…then it would be reasonable for me to be concerned."

Despite later conclusions as to the political atmosphere in the days leading up to the Iraqi invasion of Kuwait, it is probable that Saddam Hussein underestimated the resolve of the United States, Great Britain, and other Western nations, along with a host of Arab countries and the larger Coalition, to respond forcefully to his aggression. Perhaps he had misinterpreted Glaspie's statement regarding disputes between Arab countries as an assurance of non-intervention. If so, the result must indeed have been profoundly shocking. ◼

were obviously intended to galvanise the attendees in support of his intent to isolate Arab countries with friendly ties to the US, while linking them unfavourably to Israel.

On July 25, 1990, April Glaspie, the US Ambassador to Iraq, met with Saddam Hussein in Baghdad. She conveyed the message that her government wanted the simmering disputes between Middle Eastern countries to be resolved peacefully.

Saddam assumed the offensive and declared: "So what can it mean when America says it will now protect its friends? It can only mean prejudice against Iraq. This stance plus manoeuvres and statements which have been made have encouraged the United Arab Emirates and Kuwait to disregard Iraqi rights…

If you use pressure, we will deploy pressure and force. We know that you can harm us although we do not threaten you. But we too can harm you. Everyone can cause harm according to their ability and their size. We cannot come all the way to you in the United States, but individual Arabs may reach you."

Glaspie responded candidly, stating: "I know you need funds. We understand that, and in our opinion, you should have the opportunity to rebuild your country. But we have no opinion on the Arab-Arab conflicts like your border disagreement with Kuwait… Frankly we can only see that you have deployed massive troops in the south…" She went on to qualify that perspective by adding that recent statements from Saddam and his government had equated the stance

Career diplomat Tariq Aziz served as Iraqi minister of foreign affairs before and during the Gulf War. *(Creative Commons SalimIRQ via Wikimedia Commons)*

The Al Basrah oil terminal bustles with activity in this recent photograph. *(US Army Corps of Engineers via Wikimedia Commons)*

SEIZURE OF KUWAIT

in the Rumaila oil field. It was just one of their requirements to avoid military action. However, the Kuwaitis responded with an offer of only $500mn, a fraction of the dictated sum. Staring down the proverbial "barrel of a loaded gun", the Kuwaitis probably knew to a man that war was inevitable. And it was a logical but painful conclusion to months of posturing by Saddam Hussein followed by the massing of Iraqi military might on the doorstep of Kuwait.

At approximately 2am local time on August 2, 1990, the storm broke in the Middle East. Iraqi mechanised forces dashed across the Kuwaiti border and streamed into the country against only light opposition. The Iraqi army

A column of Iraqi tanks squats menacingly on a street in Kuwait City. *(Public Domain Zymogen92 via Wikimedia Commons)*

THE TWO HOURS of parlay were probably doomed from the start. On July 31, 1990, Kuwaiti Crown Prince and Prime Minister Shaikh Saad Al Abdullah Al Sabah and Izzat Ebrahim, vice chairman of the Ba'ath Party's Revolutionary Council in Iraq had come to the negotiating table in a near futile attempt to settle their countries' differences that centred on land, oil, and outstanding debt.

In the Red Sea port of Jeddah, Saudi Arabia, the delegations had been invited to discuss their opposing perspectives by Saudi King Fahd Bin Abdul Aziz, whose country also had a stake in the outcome. The two sides sometimes glared at one another, attempted to come to some arrangement, and then parted with nothing settled. Throughout the proceedings, the Iraqi diplomats had been stern and firmly asserted that their government would not tolerate further delays in the resolution of the issues at hand.

The Iraqis demanded a payment – perhaps more aptly described as an extortion – of $10bn for oil the Kuwaitis had supposedly illegally siphoned out of the ground via slant drilling

A relic of the brutal 1990 Iraqi invasion of Kuwait, this Iraqi Type 69 tank is now a museum piece in Kuwait City.
(Public Domain Arwcheek via Wikimedia Commons)

This Soviet-built Mi-24 attack helicopter, used by Iraqi forces during the invasion of Kuwait, was later captured by Coalition forces in Operation Desert Storm. *(US Air Force via Wikimedia Commons)*

was perhaps the fourth largest in the world with nearly a million men under arms, some of them veterans of the bloody war with Iran, while an auxiliary paramilitary complement numbered well over 600,000. Its Soviet-built armoured component numbered roughly 5,500 tanks, and its air force possessed over 700 fixed-wing and rotor-powered attack and transport aircraft. For the undertaking of Project 17, as the Iraqi military had code-named the invasion, 140,000 soldiers and 1,800 tanks had been prepositioned.

In sharp contrast, the diminutive Kuwaiti army numbered about 20,000 troops, many of them unprepared or minimally trained to contend with such a daunting enemy. Only about 350 tanks were available, and the air force was relatively small too.

Although Iraqi special forces and infiltrators had already undertaken offensive operations, the sledgehammer fell when four combat divisions of the elite Republican Guard, the 1st Hammurabi Armoured, 2nd al-Medinah al Munawera, 4th Nebuchadnezzar motorised infantry, and Tawakalna ala-Allah motorised infantry, rolled forward with another special forces contingent equivalent to division strength in direct support. Fighters and ground attack planes ranged overhead along with heavily armed Soviet-built tank-killing helicopters. Transport helicopters delivered special forces directly into the capital of Kuwait City. Heavy bombing raids against Kuwaiti air bases neutralised many French-built Mirage and American Douglas A-4 fighter planes on the ground. Roughly 20% of the Kuwaiti air force was destroyed, while the remainder fled to bases in Saudi Arabia and Bahrain.

Surprisingly, though war was imminent, the Kuwaiti army was apparently not on full alert. Confusion spread rapidly amid radar-generated reports that a full-scale invasion was underway. Elements of the 35th Brigade rallied to offer some resistance against the marauding Iraqis. With a battalion of Chieftain tanks, armoured personnel carriers, and a single battery of artillery, these Kuwaitis fought

Iraqi T-72 tanks like these were a mainstay of Saddam Hussein's armoured force during the Gulf War. *(US Navy via Wikimedia Commons)*

These Kuwaiti M84 tanks were photographed before the outbreak of hostilities with Iraq. *(US Army via Wikimedia Commons)*

the Battle of the Bridges in one of the few significant instances of organised resistance.

At the junction of Highway 70 and the Sixth Ring Road near the town of Al Jahra in western Kuwait, the Kuwaitis fought elements of both the Hammurabi and al-Medinah divisions. Although the defenders inflicted heavy casualties, they were eventually forced to withdraw south to avoid being overwhelmed or encircled as ammunition ran low. When the way forward was cleared, the Iraqis had lost an unknown number of men and machines. The remnants of the 35th Brigade were reported to have retreated to the Saudi border by late afternoon and then crossed over to sanctuary the following morning.

Further south, the Kuwaiti 15th Armoured Brigade moved towards Saudi Arabia as well rather than face probable annihilation. Elsewhere, pockets of dedicated resistance slowed the invaders at times, but the mobile Iraqi spearheads regularly bypassed these obstacles, allowing follow-on formations to reduce them, and sped virtually unimpeded along the highway 80 miles towards Kuwait City, which they reached within a matter of hours.

A pitched battle took place at Dasman Palace, the royal residence of the Emir of Kuwait in

This Kuwaiti M84 tank survived the initial Iraqi onslaught to serve during Operation Desert Shield/Storm. *(US Air Force via Wikimedia Commons)*

the capital city. Iraqi special forces attacked the palace around 4am, and were joined by infiltrators that had made their way to the location dressed as civilians. Fighting raged for approximately ten hours. The initial Iraqi assault was thrown back as the palace guard was joined by a few Chieftain and M84 tanks, and Saladin armoured cars. (The M84 was a Yugoslav-built variant of the Soviet-designed T-72.)

As the emir and his entourage fled to safety in Saudi Arabia by helicopter, the fighting at the palace intensified. The emir's half-brother was shot dead during a deadly exchange of small-arms fire. His corpse was reported to have been placed before the treads of an Iraqi tank and crushed in a grisly spectacle. Iraqi amphibious forces landed nearby, exerting further pressure on the defenders, and soon enough the Republican Guard leading elements began to arrive. The eventual outcome of the Battle of Dasman Palace was never in doubt. However, the glimmer of Kuwaiti valour there,

A T-72 of the Iraqi Republican Guard is shown during the invasion of Kuwait. *(Government of Iraq via Wikimedia Commons)*

and in other locations, did inspire a later resistance to the brutal occupation that followed.

In less than 24 hours, organised Kuwaiti resistance had been reduced substantially. Here and there, pockets of diehard defenders held on until eliminated. The fighting was largely over and the country was prostrate before its conquerors within two days. Estimates of casualties on both sides appear relatively light – due primarily to the lightning quickness of the Iraqi onslaught. Iraqi casualties are estimated at fewer than 600 killed and wounded, while the Kuwaitis lost roughly 400 dead along with several thousand taken prisoner.

In the immediate aftermath of the fighting, a Kuwaiti resistance movement took shape as civilians, with little in the way of military training, organised to oppose the aggressors while pamphlets were printed to bolster the morale of the citizenry now under occupation.

This Bell 214ST transport helicopter of the Iraqi Air Force was manufactured in the United States. *(US Army via Wikimedia Commons)*

Kuwaiti soldiers rest beside an armoured personnel carrier during the fight to liberate their country. *(US Marine Corps via Wikimedia Commons)*

British-built Chieftain tanks such as this example at the Bovington Museum, were fielded by the Kuwaiti army in 1990. *(Creative Commons Andrew Skudder via Wikimedia Commons)*

including incubators that kept newborn babies alive. Horrific reports of the babies being removed and then physically smashed into adjacent walls by rampaging Iraqi soldiers or left to die on the cold floor surfaced. Cancer patients were denied continuing treatment.

The national treasury of Kuwait was emptied of $4bn in gold and currency, while infrastructure, including wire and lengths of pipe, were taken away. Virtually anything of value was removed – a justifiable repayment, as Saddam Hussein's government perceived, for the wrongs done to the Iraqi people. Along with the removal of telecommunications networks, construction equipment, kitchen appliances, and even traffic signal lights, came a concerted effort to erase the vestiges of Kuwaiti national identity.

Art museums were plundered, and precious objects of antiquity were stolen, many of them destined to end up circulating on the global black market where dealers, collectors, and even other museums paid well and did not ask questions. In Washington, DC, Sheikha Hussa Sabah Al-Salem Al-Sabh broke down in tears as she described the wholesale ransacking of her country's heritage. She described the loss of "unique pieces that cannot be replaced" and lamented the loss of the treasures as the "loss of the country".

News flashes of Iraqi brutality were broadcast around the world, and civilised nations recoiled at the reports. For some of the Kuwaiti people, the nightmare was even worse. During seven months of Iraqi occupation, at least 250 women were raped by soldiers. Some of these victims were ultimately driven to suicide. Others were

The resistance received some covert aid from the US Central Intelligence Agency and the American military, but the Iraqi secret police and armed forces were constantly hunting these valiant few and then dispensing cruel justice – often in the streets of cities and towns where the local population was terrorised by these scenes of mass executions.

Such summary justice was only one facet of the heavy-handed Iraqi seizure, exploitation, and rape of the Kuwaiti nation. The Iraqi brutalisation of Kuwait may be mentioned without hesitation as comparable to the Japanese devastation of Nanking in 1937 during the Second Sino-Japanese War, and other odious examples of mankind's 20th century inhumanity to mankind.

Massive portraits of a devilishly smiling Saddam Hussein were mounted in public places. Kuwaitis were obliged to surrender their identity documents, trading them for Iraqi papers. Homes were stripped of furnishings, electronics,

and even clothing as these were loaded aboard trucks, automobiles, and even taxis headed back to Iraq with ill-gotten booty. Businesses and government buildings were looted, and anything of value was confiscated as spoils of war. Hospitals were emptied of equipment,

Two Kuwaiti soldiers run for the cover of a trench during Operation Desert Shield. *(US Air Force via Wikimedia Commons)*

A Kuwaiti soldier poses for a camera shot during Operation Desert Storm. *(Public Domain XxMWIIxX via Wikimedia Commons)*

This damaged building in Kuwait City bears the scars of the Iraqi invasion and occupation. *(US Army via Wikimedia Commons)*

Broken windows evidence the damage done in Kuwait City during the Iraqi invasion of 1990. *(US Department of Defense via Wikimedia Commons)*

resigned to bear the emotional and physical scars of those dark days for the rest of their lives.

When Amnesty International published a survey of the debacle in Kuwait in December 1990, confronting the Iraqi ambassador to Britain with evidence of his country's misdeeds, the diplomat could only answer that the Iraqi people were suffering from the effects of international embargoes of goods imposed by Coalition nations.

A New York-based human rights group issued a report on the devastation of Kuwait in the autumn of 1990 and noted: "Summary executions of scores of people have been carried out in detention centres and in public, in front of their families. Families are being terrorised by midnight searchers and arbitrary arrests of close to 5,000 people – including children. Detainees are subjected to torture and kept in crowded and unsanitary conditions, without access to families or lawyers, and without opportunity for trial. Collective punishment is meted out in response to acts of armed resistance: houses are burned, buildings demolished, curfews imposed, and families of suspects detained. Occupation authorities interfere with food distribution, warehouses are seized, food co-operatives plundered, and food distribution volunteers detained, terrorised, and in some cases executed."

Relief agencies were regularly refused access to the occupied country. They were not allowed to administer aid to the destitute or to deliver supplies. Even the International Red Cross was forbidden to intervene. The Iraqis systematically perpetrated crimes against humanity on a massive scale in a seven-month orgy of retaliation, retribution, revenge, and outright murder.

Richard Curtiss, a retired Foreign Service officer and editor of the *Washington Report on Middle Eastern Affairs*, a respected American journal focusing on US policy in the Middle East, was aghast when he arrived in Kuwait City after the Gulf War was over.

"Just total devastation! That's how I would describe it," Curtiss assessed. "I couldn't help thinking 'but I've seen all of this on television. I've watched the CNN reports that graphically displayed the destruction of the capital'. However, you can't really feel that total destruction that is 360-degrees around you. If you ask the Kuwaitis about the unspeakable atrocities they endured for seven months, of course, each has a story to tell."

The rest of the world did not sit idly by while Iraqi soldiers raped and pillaged in Kuwait. An effective and decisive response was in the offing, first in the form of widespread denunciation of blatant Iraqi aggression, then with the tightening of already imposed stinging economic sanctions, and finally with the might of a vengeful military alliance that would eventually liberate the oppressed and brutalised Kuwaiti people and restore the rightful government in the country.

However, during the intervening time, the devil himself appeared on the loose in the Middle East. Without remorse or pity, Saddam Hussein had dared to cross the line from rhetoric to outright military confrontation. ◼

A number of Kuwaiti Air Force fighters like this Douglas A-4 Skyhawk were destroyed on the ground during the Iraqi invasion of August 1990. *(US Navy via Wikimedia Commons)*

Surrounded by advisors, President Bush and Prime Minister Thatcher confer in the Oval Office at the White House on August 6, 1990. *(George Bush Presidential Library and Museum via Wikimedia Commons)*

INTERNATIONAL
CONDEMNATION

WHEN THE THREAT of Iraqi aggression became real on August 2, 1990, the initial response around the world was one of shock. Saddam Hussein had made good on his threat of military action to gain full control of what he believed was the "19th province" of his country unjustly taken away by the British government decades earlier and made a separate protectorate.

President George H W Bush was in Aspen, Colorado, along with Prime Minister Margaret Thatcher, attending a 40th anniversary symposium at the Aspen Institute when they received the news. They convened a joint press conference to set the stage for a firm and immediate international response.

The President commented: "Let me first welcome Prime Minister Thatcher back to the United States. It is a very timely visit and as you can well imagine we have been exchanging views on the Iraq-Kuwait situation. Not surprisingly, I find myself very much in accord with the views of the Prime Minister."

Bush went on to indicate that he had already made contact with King Hussein of Jordan, President Hosni Mubarak of Egypt, President Sallah of Yemen, King Fahd of Saudi Arabia, and other world leaders. "I can tell you that Jim Baker (US Secretary of State) has been in close touch with the Soviet leadership and indeed the last plan was for him to stop in Moscow on his way back here. We are concerned about the situation but I find that Prime Minister Thatcher and I are looking at it on exactly the same wavelength: concern about this naked aggression, condemning it

Tariq Aziz and Saddam Hussein attend the Arab League summit in Amman, Jordan, in 1980. *(Government of Iraq via Wikimedia Commons)*

President Bush and Japanese Prime Minister Toshiki Kaifu greet the media after a 1990 conference. *(George Bush Presidential Library and Museum via Wikimedia Commons)*

President Bush and Soviet leader Mikhail Gorbachev pause for photographers at the Helsinki summit, September 1990. *(George Bush Presidential Library and Museum via Wikimedia Commons)*

and hoping that a peaceful solution will be found that will result in the restoration of the Kuwaiti leaders to their rightful place and prior to that a withdrawal of Iraqi forces."

Margaret Thatcher forcefully added: "Iraq has violated and taken over the territory of a country which is a full member of the United Nations. That is totally unacceptable and if it were allowed to endure, then there would be many other small countries that could never feel safe. The Security Council acted swiftly last night under United States leadership, well supported by the votes of 14 members of the Security Council, and rightly demanded the withdrawal of Iraqi troops.

"If the withdrawal is not swiftly forthcoming," she continued, "we have to consider the next step. The next step would be further consideration by the Security Council of possible measures under Chapter 7. The fundamental question is this: whether the nations of the world have the collective will effectively to see that the Security Council resolution is upheld, whether they have the collective will effectively to do anything which the Security Council further agrees

Soviet leader Mikhail Gorbachev listens to an interpreter in Helsinki. His support was critical to the Coalition formation. *(George Bush Presidential Library and Museum via Wikimedia Commons)*

With the news of the Iraqi invasion of Kuwait breaking, President Bush and Prime Minister Thatcher address reporters in Aspen, Colorado. *(Records of the White House Photograph Office via Wikimedia Commons)*

to see that Iraq withdraws and that the government of Kuwait is restored to Kuwait."

Indeed, hours earlier, the United Nations Security Council had acted under Chapter 7 of the UN Charter, passing Resolution 660 that condemned the invasion of Kuwait and demanded the immediate and unconditional withdrawal of Iraqi forces from that country. Four days later, the Security Council took further steps to exert pressure on Saddam Hussein. Resolution 661 levied comprehensive economic sanctions and an extensive trade embargo against Iraq following the defiance expressed by the Baghdad government and noncompliance with Resolution 660.

US Ambassador to the United Nations Thomas Pickering remembered the moment that his dinner was interrupted and he began the push for UN action. "I was called out of the dining room by the waiter to take an urgent call from the State Department. I took it in the pantry with all the waiters running around. I talked

to Bob Kimmett (Under Secretary for Political Affairs) and we talked a little bit about the character of the resolution they were working on for the Security Council in New York."

The pace of the response to Iraq's aggression quickened. On August 3, the US and Soviet governments had presented a co-operative posture to the rest of the world. Soviet leader Mikhail Gorbachev had weighed the cost-benefit of maintaining his country's longstanding ties to Iraq and the obvious aggression that country had committed. His conclusion reinforced the momentum of the worldwide groundswell in opposition to Saddam's military action and the detaining of many Westerners who had been living and working in Kuwait. While Secretary Jim Baker flew from meetings in Mongolia to Moscow for discussions, the Soviets announced a suspension of all arms deliveries to the Baghdad government. At the same time, the United States imposed its own embargo on oil and trade to Iraq. The US and French governments announced the freezing of Iraqi and Kuwaiti assets within their countries.

Two days later, President Bush illustrated the burgeoning global co-operation in confronting Iraq. From the South Lawn of the White House on August 5, he told reporters: "I just wanted to fill you all in on the diplomatic activity that is taking place – intensive diplomatic activity around the world. I'm getting another call from President Özal of Turkey… I talked this morning to Prime Minister Kaifu, and I applaud Japan's stance cracking down on the imports from Iraq. I just hung up, up there in Camp David, talking with Prime Minister Mulroney [Canada]. We're all in the same accord – he and President Mitterand [France], with whom I've spoken, Chancellor Kohl [Germany], Margaret Thatcher. I think the alliance, the NATO alliance, is thinking exactly the same way on this. I also talked yesterday to Kuwait's Emir and gave him certain assurances…"

Bush concluded his remarks with the now famous declaration: "This will not stand. This will not stand, this aggression against Kuwait."

Meanwhile, amid continuing discussions with world leaders, President Bush and King Fahd of Saudi Arabia measured the threat of widening Iraqi military activity. The Saudi ruler and the United States reached an agreement to send American forces to the oil-rich country as a defensive measure to deter such an event.

The rhetoric from Baghdad was predictable as Saddam Hussein sought to drive a wedge between Western countries and the Arab nations that surrounded Iraq. Saddam's Foreign Minister Tariq Aziz refused to characterise the detainees inside Kuwait, whose numbers were estimated at about 5,000 and could potentially be used as human shields, as hostages. He laughed at a reporter's inquiry: "Hostages, my dear friend, don't live in hotels, talk to their relatives in the US and Britain, enjoy life better than we do. They are not hostages – they are guests."

The bombastic Iraqi leader exhorted other Arabs to side with his country, attempting to justify the occupation of Kuwait as a liberation and a stand against non-Islamic influence. He proclaimed a holy war as US

President Bush, Prime Minister Thatcher, and NATO Secretary General Manfred Woerner answer questions on the deepening crisis in the Middle East at the White House on August 6, 1990. *(George Bush Presidential Library and Museum via Wikimedia Commons)*

troops headed to Saudi Arabia, allegedly desecrating the land of the two holiest sites in Islam, Mecca and Medina, and tried to drag Israel into the swirling crisis.

"Oh Arabs, oh Muslims and faithful everywhere, this is your day to rise and defend Mecca, which is captured by the spears of the Americans and the Zionists," Saddam bellowed. "Burn the land under the feet of the aggressors who want evil for the people of Iraq, after which their weakness will spread in the whole Arab world. Hit their interests wherever they are… Iraq has insisted on a holy war without hesitation or retreat against the foreign forces until you reach heaven or martyrdom."

Saddam's outcry was ringing in the ears of the delegates to the emergency summit of the Arab League held in the Egyptian capital of Cairo on August 10. Twenty of the 21 League nations were represented during the fiery meeting. It was reported that Kuwaiti Foreign Minister Sheikh Sabah al Ahmed al Sabah actually fainted after

US Secretary of State James Baker was a key participant in the early response to the Iraqi invasion of Kuwait. *(U.S. Department of State)*

an exchange with Tariq Aziz, and that Iraqi delegates hurled plates of food at the Kuwaitis in attendance during a lunch break.

In the end, 12 Arab nations not only chose to reinforce a resolution condemning the Iraqi invasion that had been issued by their foreign ministers a week earlier, but also adopted a resolution to send troops from member nations to Saudi Arabia and other nations of the Persian Gulf region that were threatened. The measure was approved on the heels of Iraq's firm refusal to negotiate a peaceful withdrawal of its forces from Kuwait. Those nations voting in favour of the resolution were Saudi Arabia, Egypt, Djibouti, Kuwait, Bahrain, the United Arab Emirates, Syria, Somalia, Oman, Qatar, Morocco, and Lebanon. Libya and Iraq voted against the resolution, while Yemen and Algeria abstained, and Sudan, Mauritania, and most notably Jordan voiced "reservations" against such emphatic action. Tunisia did not send a representative to the proceedings.

Three days before the Arab League summit, President Bush had issued orders

US Secretary of Defense Dick Cheney and King Fahd of Saudi Arabia discuss the situation in the Middle East in late 1990. *(US Department of Defense via Wikimedia Commons)*

Secretary of State James Baker meets with President Bush on August 8, 1990, as the crisis in Kuwait deepens. *(George Bush Presidential Library and Museum via Wikimedia Commons)*

Libyan strongman Muammar Khadafi meets with Ali Abdullah Saleh, president of Yemen, in 1990. At the Arab summit in Cairo, Libya voted against action on Iraq while Yemen abstained. *(Saba News Agency via Wikimedia Commons)*

to begin the buildup of US forces in the Middle East, particularly Saudi Arabia, that initiated Operation Desert Shield.

On September 9, 1990, Gorbachev and Bush met in Helsinki, Finland, to discuss the deepening crisis in the Middle East. The hope for a diplomatic solution was fading, although every effort was being made, short of military action, to persuade the Iraqi government to withdraw from Kuwait. At the conclusion of their summit, the leaders issued a two-page joint statement:

"We are united in the belief that Iraq's aggression will not be tolerated. No peaceful international order is possible if larger states can devour their smaller neighbours...Today, we once again call upon the government of Iraq to withdraw unconditionally from Kuwait, to allow the restoration of Kuwait's legitimate government, and to free all hostages now held in Iraq and Kuwait."

As efforts to reach a diplomatic solution to the deepening emergency seemed futile, the international military Coalition began taking shape. At first the introduction of forces, which soon would include a contingent of 5,000 Egyptian soldiers headed to Saudi Arabia, was intended for defensive purposes. However, as the weeks wore on, the posture evolved. On November 29, the United Nations passed Resolution 678 authorising member nations to implement "all necessary means" to eject Iraqi forces from Kuwait if the deadline of January 15, 1991, was not met. ∎

World leaders who later condemned the Iraqi invasion of Kuwait gather for an economic summit in Houston, Texas, in the summer of 1990. *(Records of the White House Photograph Office via Wikimedia Commons)*

INTELLIGENCE – EYES AND EARS

FIRST THERE WAS a warning of clear and present danger. Whether the leaders of the civilised nations of the world took heed or not, the evidence was there. Although the Iraqi invasion of Kuwait came as a profound surprise to many, it was not because of an outright intelligence failure but more accurately due to a failure to interpret the signs of impending military action.

A modified KC-135 tanker derived from the Boeing 707 passenger liner, the E-3 Sentry AWACS monitored Iraqi aircraft activity. *(US Air Force via Wikimedia Commons)*

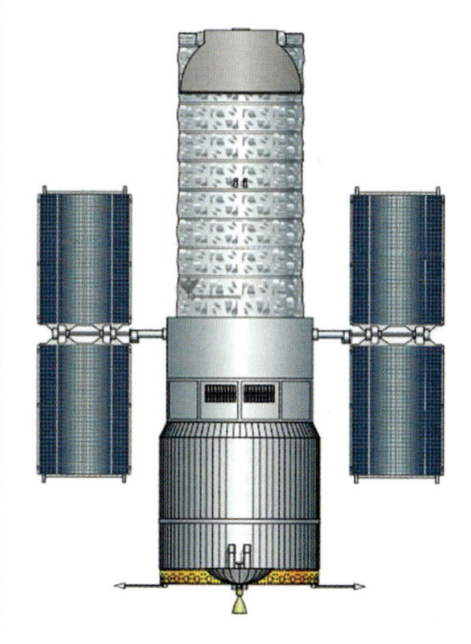

**KH-11
KENNEN
(1976-Ogoing)**

The KH-11 KENNEN satellite was instrumental in gathering intelligence on Iraqi dispositions. *(Creative Commons Giuseppe De Chiara 1968 via Wikimedia Commons)*

While Saddam Hussein bloviated and blustered, his armed forces were mobilised. And when American satellite surveillance delivered startling images of at least 100,000 Iraqi soldiers, hundreds of tanks, armoured personnel carriers, artillery pieces, and supply and logistics support massed near the border with Kuwait, the implication might have been clear. However, Arab and Western leaders chose to chalk the provocation up to more sabre rattling, rhetoric and threats.

Even so, when the Iraqi forces swarmed into Kuwait on August 2, 1990, the tools of intelligence had already been providing vital information to those who would craft the armed response, building the great Coalition of Desert Shield, and then unleashing the retribution of Desert Storm.

Modern technology and boots on the ground combined to present perhaps the clearest picture in history of the strategic and tactical challenges that confronted a commander, and General Norman Schwarzkopf, and other military men, took full advantage of the situation. The blinders that inhibited a forceful response were removed, allowing the planning and execution of Desert Storm to be unrivalled in the history of military operations.

On multiple levels, the eyes and ears of the Coalition were at work, pinpointing Iraqi assets and doing so in ways never before seen in warfare. The use of satellites was primary, while spy planes flew literally into the stratosphere and tactical aircraft performed reconnaissance missions to deliver photo intelligence, or PHOTINT. Meanwhile, eavesdropping was continuous as Iraqi communications via telephone and other means was readily intercepted and analysed. From communications intelligence, or COMINT, valuable information was gleaned. Electronic emissions intelligence, ELINT, read the signatures of Iraqi radar apparatus, and human intelligence, HUMINT, men in harm's way, conducted covert surveillance in enemy territory at great risk but with tangible results.

Through these four elements of intelligence gathering, Coalition forces pierced the veil of secrecy, erased much of the unknown regarding the strength and dispositions of Iraqi assets, and proceeded to conduct combat operations on land, sea, and air that produced the eventual victory. Finding and fixing the enemy were prerequisites to destroying his military capabilities, and in that endeavour the Gulf War was historic in its precision and ultimate success.

United States Central Command was charged first with the mission of containing the Iraqis in Kuwait, preventing the widening of the rogue

The Lacrosse satellite brought a new generation of technology to the Gulf War. *(National Reconnaissance Office via Wikimedia Commons)*

Nicknamed 'Dragon Lady', the Lockheed U-2 spy plane was a true eye in the sky for the Coalition. *(US Air Force via Wikimedia Commons)*

The McDonnell Douglas RF-4C Phantom II was the reconnaissance version of the F-4 Phantom fighter. *(US Air Force via Wikimedia Commons)*

country's military ambitions to Saudi Arabia, and later developed into offensive action to eject the aggressor from Kuwait entirely.

Early in the process, the Coalition relied on satellite photo reconnaissance, and a trio of the most advanced systems of their kind were already in orbit. Capable of standing vigil across the globe, these modern marvels were a pair of KH-11 satellites, nicknamed 'Keyhole', and the more recently deployed Lacrosse satellite system. The KH-11 KENNEN was manufactured by Lockheed and launched by the American National Reconnaissance Office in December 1976 as the first satellite to utilise electro-optical visual imaging and transmit real-time optical observations. Also developed by Lockheed, Lacrosse was deployed in December 1988 by the Space Shuttle Atlantis.

Both Keyhole and Lacrosse were manoeuvred to make the Middle East, namely Iraq and Kuwait, the focus of their intelligence gathering. Aboard the KH-11's advanced technology included the

A soldier of the Coalition special forces inspects an abandoned Iraqi trench. *(US Department of Defense via Wikimedia Commons)*

light-sensitive video charge coupled device (CCD) which employed semiconductors and pixels in synthesising up to 640,000 photo elements in extensive images transmitted through a tracking system or relay satellite to analysts in Washington, DC For its time, the accuracy of the images was remarkable, allowing

the identification of objects just a few feet in length from a distance of 100 miles. Although KH-11 images could distinguish between tanks, artillery pieces, buildings, and other structures, the system's ability to penetrate cloud cover was limited. The next generation Lacrosse carried synthetic aperture radar (SAR), which pierced the smoke and atmospheric interference with its huge antenna, stretching 12ft by 48ft, in either single still photographic evidence or in a phased sweep of an extensive area. In tandem, these satellites sent updated information on Iraqi dispositions twice each day.

Manned aircraft performed essential reconnaissance too. Already famed after three decades of service, the U-2 spy plane, developed by the covert Lockheed Skunk Works in Burbank, California, in the 1950s, completed multiple missions utilising its sophisticated camera equipment to take detailed photographs of territory at a distance of 50 miles or more. At the same time, the reconnaissance version of the

No Coalition aircraft were lost to enemy SAMs during Desert Storm when the EF-111A Raven was in the air. *(US Government via Wikimedia Commons)*

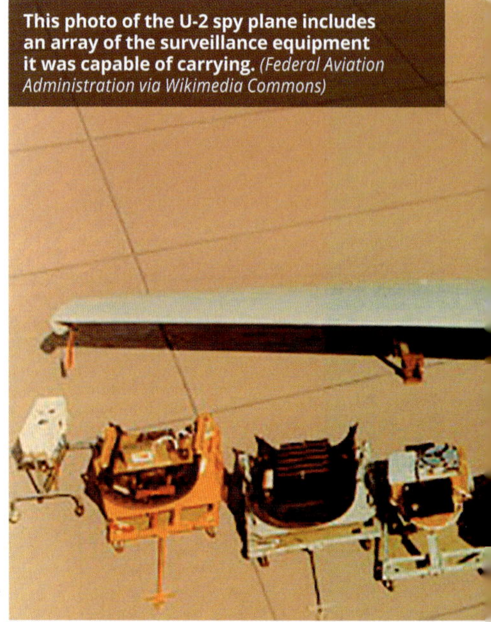

This photo of the U-2 spy plane includes an array of the surveillance equipment it was capable of carrying. *(Federal Aviation Administration via Wikimedia Commons)*

The Grumman EA-6B Prowler was an effective electronic warfare aircraft during Desert Storm.
(US Marine Corps via Wikimedia Commons)

McDonnell Douglas F-4 Phantom fighter joined in. The RF-4C Phantom II streaked above enemy-occupied territory, its four cameras whirring with frames from forward, oblique, and vertical angles. Although the U-2 flew at such altitude that the threat of Iraqi surface-to-air missiles (SAM) was greatly diminished, the Phantoms were typically flown at lower altitudes, and pilots and weapons system operators were at times alarmed by radar lock-on warning tones, visual sightings of SAM launches or actual missiles in flight, and even the concussions of near-misses.

Other air surveillance assets included the big EC-130H Compass Call variant of the Lockheed C-130 Hercules transport. The EC-130H carried equipment that monitored Iraqi radio communications, located the position of the source, and facilitated later combat missions that destroyed the sites or jammed their efforts to co-ordinate between enemy command and control centres and units in the field. Further, the famed E-3 AWACS Sentry (airborne warning and control system) surveillance aircraft, identifiable with its large circular radome, kept watch over Iraqi airfields and installations, swiftly reporting any enemy aircraft that took to the sky.

Further tactical air surveillance and detection was conducted by the US Navy's EA-6B Prowler, the electronic warfare variant of the Grumman A-6 Intruder carrier-based attack aircraft, and the EF-111A Raven, the surveillance version of the General Dynamics F-111 medium-range fighter bomber, which pinpointed Iraqi SAM sites and effectively jammed radar transmissions as combat aircraft were vectored in to deal with the threat to Coalition planes. Comprehensive ELINT was a priority before and during the Desert Shield buildup and Desert Storm combat actions.

The importance of HUMINT can never be minimised, and during Desert Shield/Storm it took several forms. Soon after the Iraqi occupation of their country, Kuwaiti resistance personnel risked their lives in cities and towns across their own territory, and even infiltrated into Iraq to gather information on Saddam's military strength and locations. Kurdish fighters, long opposed to the Ba'athist regime in Baghdad, co-operated with the Coalition, providing information from inside Iraq. When telephone communication lines between Kuwait and Saudi Arabia were cut, cellular technology was employed.

Covert military operations were set in motion against the Iraqis as Coalition special forces teams of the US Army, Navy, and Air Force, and the British Special Air Service were inserted by helicopter and rode across the desert in "dune buggies" officially known as Fast Attack Vehicles (FAV) or Desert Patrol Vehicles (DPV). These intrepid units located Iraqi Scud missile and SAM sites, troop and armour concentrations, and other high value targets, concealing themselves from detection and disrupting enemy operations wherever possible.

The Coalition intelligence advantage was decisive during the Gulf War, and no doubt saved lives in the execution of Desert Storm. ◼

CONSENSUS AND DISSENT

WHILE MOST OF the world openly criticised and condemned Saddam Hussein and Iraq for its aggression against Kuwait, there were some nations that were reluctant supporters, neutral if such was even possible, or offered support reluctantly.

Among the Arab nations there were mixed sentiments. Opposition to Israel was a driver of foreign policy in most cases, while economic, religious, territorial, and ancestral ties were also contributing factors. Chief among those Arab countries that did not readily join the Coalition was the Kingdom of Jordan, led by King Hussein.

The Jordanian delegation to the emergency Arab League summit in Cairo in August 1990 had declined to support resolutions condemning the Iraqi invasion of Kuwait or the mobilisation of troops to defend countries threatened by any widening aggression by Saddam's regime. Jordan had, in recent years, oriented its foreign policy towards the West, while Iraq had relied on economic and military support from the Soviet Union. However, this circumstance had come about chiefly after the 1958 military coup that toppled Iraq's King Faisal II just six months after Jordan and Iraq had come together to form the Hashemite Arab Federation.

The two countries, both established under British mandate after World War One, shared their early rulers' Hashemite heritage. Brothers Abdullah and Faisal, sons of Sharif Hussein ibn Ali, had been placed on the thrones of Jordan and Iraq respectively, and both rulers claimed descent from the prophet Muhammed through his great grandfather, Hashim. Even though the coup had ended Hashemite rule in Iraq, the two nations shared further common ties.

By the 1970s, Saddam Hussein and King Hussein, both Sunni Muslims, had forged a

King Hussein of Jordan attempted to mediate the crisis in the Persian Gulf but failed. *(US Department of Defense via Wikimedia Commons)*

personal friendship and developed extensive economic interdependence. The 1979 Iranian Revolution was considered a mutual threat, drawing them even closer. During the 1980-88 war with Iran, Jordan was a significant supporter of Saddam's embattled regime, providing military aid and even some ground troops to Iraq. Jordan served as a significant economic partner to Iraq in those troubled years, allowing import and export traffic via the port of Aqaba in exchange for Iraqi oil at a discounted price. By 1990, Iraq had become Jordan's largest export market.

Therefore, the countries were drawn together by the common threat from Iran, economic necessity, and their significant religious heritage. In 1989, Jordan and Iraq had joined the Arab Co-operation Council, along with Egypt and North Yemen. However, the organisation withered in the wake of the Iraqi invasion of Kuwait the following year.

King Hussein responded quickly to the surprising news that Iraq had invaded Kuwait and informed the US government within hours that he intended to travel to Baghdad to hopefully broker a peaceful solution to the crisis with Saddam Hussein. The face-to-face discussion took place on August 3, 1990, only a day after the invasion, and the Iraqi leader was firm in his stance that no withdrawal would take place if other Arab nations condemned the aggression or authorised foreign troops to intervene. However, early statements issued by other Arab countries, as well as the decisions at the Arab League summit, undermined the Jordanian leader's effort to further mediate.

During the Arab League summit, Jordanian Foreign Minister Marwan Al-Kasim warned that condemnation of Iraq would diminish the prospects for a peaceful end to the crisis. His entreaties fell on deaf ears, some

Shown near the end of his rule in Libya, Moammar Khadafi opposed Western influence in the Middle East. *(Government of the Russian Federation via Wikimedia Commons)*

King Hussein greets Saddam Hussein during a state visit to Jordan in February 1990. *(Government of Iraq via Wikimedia Commons)*

King Hussein of Jordan and King Faisal II of Iraq are pictured in the early days of their reigns. *(Government of Iraq via Wikimedia Commons)*

observers attributing the situation to suspicions shared by the Kuwaitis and Saudis who distrusted the Jordanians and believed that King Hussein was vying for a share of the ill-gotten spoils of Iraq's military move.

The situation rapidly spiralled out of King Hussein's control as the first American troops arrived in Saudi Arabia on August 6. Two days later, Saddam Hussein formally annexed Kuwait and declared that the new condition could not be reversed. Even though Jordan did refuse to recognise the annexation officially, the US government saw King Hussein's position as anti-Coalition and suspended millions of dollars in economic aid to the country. In short order, other Arab states followed, further isolating Jordan in its tepid support for Iraq.

Nevertheless, King Hussein visited no fewer than a dozen nations during August-September 1990 in further efforts to defuse the situation. He did play a key role in convincing Saddam Hussein to release Western citizens who had been caught up in the recent seizure of Kuwait and had been held as hostages, bargaining chips against immediate military retaliation. One of King Hussein's last

US Secretary of State James Baker and Soviet Foreign Minister Eduard Shevardnadze confer in the White House Cabinet Room in June 1990. *(US Government via Wikimedia Commons)*

King Hussein meets with President Bush at the White House in 1992. *(Records of the White House Photographic Office via Wikimedia Commons)*

stops in his shuttle diplomacy effort was back in Baghdad. In a frank meeting with Saddam Hussein, he warned: "Make a brave decision and withdraw your forces; if you don't you will be forced out."

Afterwards, the tenor of Jordanian policy towards Iraq was altered somewhat. Jordan joined in economic sanctions against Iraq, and King Hussein ordered troops and tanks to the countries' common border. The Gulf War soon produced significant economic hardship for Jordan as an estimated 400,000 Kuwaitis became refugees in the country, costing millions, while revenues once derived from commerce with Iraq were strangled.

Libya was pro-Iraq throughout the rising crisis as its leader Moammar Khadafi shared vehement anti-Western sentiments with Saddam Hussein's Ba'athist regime. Libya had already been identified by the US as a state sponsor of terrorism, and on at least four occasions in the 1980s the two nations had nearly gone to war. In fact, American fighters had shot down four Iraqi planes and destroyed elements of the Iraqi navy in separate incidents, while American bombers had raided Tripoli, the Libyan capital, in retaliation for a disco bombing in Berlin, West Germany, that had killed three American soldiers.

Pictured in 1972, Colonel Moammar Khadafi of Libya was a principal adversary of the United States in the Middle East and northern Africa. *(Creative Commons Stevan Kragujevic via Wikimedia Commons)*

Khadafi opposed the Arab League resolutions and the introduction of foreign military assets in the Middle East as tantamount to an American seizure and exploitation of Arab resources there, and on the continent of Africa.

Elsewhere, there were rumours that the government of North Korea, which had supported Iran in its eight-year war with Iraq, actually supplied Scud missiles to Saddam Hussein.

For the Soviet Union, the situation in the Persian Gulf was vexing, having come during a most difficult period in its own history. The Soviet government had been embroiled in the collapse of communism among satellite states in Eastern Europe, and its own grip on power was decidedly slipping. In December 1991, just months after the Gulf War ended, the Soviet Union officially collapsed when Mikhail Gorbachev resigned the post of president on Christmas Day and its parliament voted to dissolve the nation less than 24 hours later.

Immediately, however, Gorbachev had issued joint statements with the US government regarding opposition to the Iraqi aggression while the Soviet leader continued to advocate for a peaceful settlement of the issue. He is said to have relied heavily on Foreign Minister Eduard Shevardnadze to quell dissent within the shaky government from officials who were inherently anti-American, and expressed concerns regarding Soviet military advisors who were still in Iraq and the loss of arms sales to Saddam's regime.

In retrospect, Shevardnadze observed that the Soviet position prior to the Gulf War devolved into one of being "informed and not consulted" by the US government. Historians have assessed the Soviet situation for what it was. After the Soviet government had been assured by Saddam Hussein that no aggression against Kuwait was forthcoming, the assurance was revealed to be a lie. In the throes of its own internal turmoil and political unrest, the Kremlin had no real alternative but to follow the US lead.

Soviet Foreign Minister Eduard Shevardnadze was his country's principal envoy during the months of Operation Desert Shield. *(US National Archives and Records Administration via Wikimedia Commons)*

Soviet policy advisor Anatoly Chernyaev bluntly noted in his diary: "...Gorbachev is reasonably saying that we cannot separate from the Americans, no matter how much we might want to avoid war. Then everything would come undone." ■

Soviet leader Mikhail Gorbachev and his wife Raisa are shown during the last days of the Soviet Union. Gorbachev had little room for diplomatic manoeuvre during the Gulf War crisis. *(Creative Commons Dumay Olivier Victor Marius via Wikimedia Commons)*

THE DESTINATION FOR
MILITARY ENTHUSIASTS

Visit us today and discover all our latest releases

Order from our online shop today...
shop.keypublishing.com
Call +44 (0)1780 480404 *(Monday to Friday 9am - 5.30pm GMT)*
Free 2nd class P&P on BFPO orders. Overseas charges apply.

DESERT SHIELD – FORGING THE ALLIANCE

THE STATEMENT LIVES on in political lore – firm and fearless, even 35 years later. Both world leaders acknowledged its context.

"Remember, George, this is no time to go wobbly," declared Prime Minister Margaret Thatcher just hours after United Nations Resolution 665 had authorised a naval blockade to enforce stiff trade and economic sanctions against Saddam Hussein's Iraq. According to Thatcher, the comment was made in a telephone conversation with President Bush, who had called from his home in Kennebunkport, Maine, on August 26, 1990.

"The President agreed," Thatcher remembered. "…We were now probably going into a longish period to see whether sanctions would work and we must not let the faint hearts grow in strength. The President was worried also about the use of the port of Aqaba in Jordan to evade sanctions and I told him that I would raise the question when I saw King Hussein in a few days."

Months later, when the Gulf War was won and President Bush presented Thatcher with the

An A-10 Thunderbolt ground attack aircraft arrives in Saudi Arabia. *(US Air Force via Wikimedia Commons)*

Presidential Medal of Freedom, he considered that historic moment. "Never, ever will it be said that Margaret Thatcher went wobbly." Amid the laughter that rippled through the gathering, there was true reflection on the challenging times in confronting the Iraqi aggression against Kuwait. Whether Thatcher really worried that Bush lacked resolve and might be faltering in his steadfastness is open to interpretation. However, in action there is evidence that the President was resolute from the beginning.

After telling reporters frankly that Iraq's aggression would not stand, President Bush,

A US Navy F/A-18 Hornet fighter flies over the aircraft carrier USS *Saratoga* during Operation Desert Shield. *(US Navy via Wikimedia Commons)*

Boots on the ground in the Middle East, US Marines move out for training. *(US National Archives and Records Administration via Wikimedia Commons)*

Approximately 750,000 soldiers, sailors, and airmen, 2,780 aircraft, 3,500 tanks, thousands of artillery pieces, and hundreds of warships were arrayed against the Iraqis.

From August 2,1990, through to the end of hostilities in February 1991, Bush issued a dozen executive orders to mobilise and deploy the US armed forces and to provide necessary support for the effort. Meanwhile, Secretary of State James Baker and Secretary of Defense Dick Cheney were dispatched around the globe to seek the contributions of other countries to the Desert Shield complement. President Bush worked the telephones and met with leaders, while his deputies flew thousands of miles.

The President addressed the nation on August 8, explaining the decision to deploy American forces to the Middle East, and by that time the 82nd Airborne Division was already aboard transport aircraft destined for airfields half a world away. The aircraft carrier USS *Saratoga*'s battle group was transiting the Strait of Gibraltar to take up station in the eastern Mediterranean Sea. By early September,

An M109 self-propelled howitzer rolls off a landing ship in Saudi Arabia.
(US Government via Wikimedia Commons)

A British tractor exits a Danish cargo ship at a port in Saudi Arabia during the build-up of Desert Shield. *(US Department of Defense via Wikimedia Commons)*

in strong partnership with Thatcher and other world leaders, set about achieving the goal of removing the Iraqis from Kuwait, first through diplomatic means with UN support, economic and trade sanctions, and concurrently with the build-up of military force that, despite the best efforts of many, became the only alternative.

In the event, President Bush took virtually immediate action to position the US military to respond to further provocation by the Iraqis if it should come, particularly in the form of hostilities with Saudi Arabia. On August 2, some sources say within an hour of receiving word of the Iraqi invasion, he ordered the aircraft carrier USS *Independence* and its battle group from the Indian Ocean and the island of Diego Garcia to the Gulf of Oman. The aircraft carrier USS *Dwight Eisenhower* was dispatched from the eastern Mediterranean to the Red Sea, passing through the Suez Canal with the permission of Egyptian President Hosni Mubarak. At home, the Ready Brigade of the US Army's 82nd Airborne Division was placed on alert at its base in Fort Bragg, North Carolina.

Operation Desert Shield, the mightiest assemblage of military strength since World War Two, was underway. When it was unleashed more than five months later, it included the armed forces and other support of 42 nations.

A formation of US Marine AV-8 Harrier fighters, deployed from Arizona, flies during Desert Shield. *(US Department of Defense via Wikimedia Commons)*

A soldier of the Queen's Dragoon Guards aims his weapon downrange during Desert Shield training. *(US Department of Defense via Wikimedia Commons)*

Kuwait which never took place in the grand plan," Admiral Fry continued. "I knew where these men were, and I went around meeting with their dependents who didn't know where they were. It was stressful knowing that some observers were predicting 30% casualties, and I was telling the dependents that their loved ones were safe. The Marine demonstration off Kuwait was a feint to draw troops away from the main action, but the waters were heavily mined. And these guys were bankers from New Orleans or warehouse workers in San Francisco in civilian life. We brought them in for some training and then deployed them out there with the Marines."

While combat assets continued to arrive in theatre, 8,000 US Marines of the 4th Marine Expeditionary Brigade and the 13th Marine Expeditionary Unit, along with 10,000 sailors of the US Navy did engage in amphibious exercises dubbed Operation Imminent Thunder, conducting landings at Ras Al Ghar on the Saudi

the British military was enacting Operation Granby with elements of the 7th Armoured Brigade the first to reach the troubled region.

While the armed forces of the United States mobilised with the activation of Reserve and National Guard units, desert training became a focus. The Desert Training Center was established at Fort Irwin, California, while other facilities were dedicated to that task. In Saudi Arabia, numerous bases were built, Navy construction battalions (Seabees) and other units devoting hours to the effort. US and Egyptian forces conducted a series of military exercises codenamed Bright Star during the months of Operation Desert Shield.

US. Military Airlift Command swung into action during the massive air movement of Coalition forces, which was accompanied by the tremendous seaborne transport of men, weapons, and materiel from around the globe to the Middle East. "We essentially had a steel bridge between the East Coast of the US and Saudi Arabia," remembered Rear Admiral Robert Crates, deputy commander of the Navy's Cargo Handling Force. "We were talking about taking 95% of all cargo movement for Desert Shield and later Desert Storm being by ship, and that was true. It was a real logistics challenge."

Admiral Vance Fry commanded eight of the Navy's 14 cargo handling battalions deployed from the US, Southwest Asia, Europe, and the Pacific during Desert Shield and Desert Storm. With thousands of sailors under his command, Fry and his Combat Stevedores tackled the herculean task of loading, transporting, and offloading the materiel of war. However, he was also a prominent figure among the families of reservists called to active duty in a frightening period.

"It really was a gratifying experience in 1990-91," commented Admiral Fry. "The reserve component was called on heavily for the logistics support of the Marines and the Navy, and to see how that reserve component worked so well was tremendous. Afterward, the integrated operations of the reserve force allowed even more effective logistics support.

"As we deployed all these people, one of the most stressful things was going aboard ships with the Marines for the invasion of

Egyptian soldiers man their M113 armoured personnel carriers during a review by visiting dignitaries. *(US Air Force via Wikimedia Commons)*

British Warrior infantry fighting vehicles are gathered in the Saudi desert. *(US Department of Defense via Wikimedia Commons)*

coast of the Persian Gulf. The aircraft carrier USS *Midway* provided extensive air cover and later launched the first air strikes of the Gulf War, while the 10,000-mile ocean voyage from bases on both coasts of the United States was continual for US seaborne assets. In less than a month, at least 20 amphibious landing ships were on station in the Gulf of Oman.

The US Air Force's 1st Tactical Fighter Wing reached the Middle East on August 9, after flying 14 hours from Langley Air Force Base, Virginia, and refuelling in mid-air seven times. Within hours of arrival, pilots were aloft in theatre, flying combat air and reconnaissance patrols in their McDonnell Douglas F-15 Eagle fighters. Altogether, the Wing deployed 48 F-15s. The 36th Tactical Fighter Wing soon joined the deployment from its base in Bitburg, Germany, while the 169th Fighter Wing of the South Carolina Air National Guard and 174th Fighter Wing of the New York Air National Guard flew to forward bases at Al Kharj, Saudi Arabia. The South Carolina unit flew 24 General Dynamics F-16 Fighting Falcon multi-role aircraft, eventually completing 2,000 combat missions and dropping four million pounds of ordnance. The New Yorkers, nicknamed the 'Boys from Syracuse', flew another two dozen F-16s in extensive combat operations.

The Ready Brigade of the 82nd Airborne established a defensive perimeter around the sprawling Saudi airport at Dhahran that same day. By the 13th, the entire brigade had deployed and a second airborne brigade was en route. When the ground force deployment crested, approximately 534,000 of the Coalition troops in the Middle East were American.

By mid-November, the UK had dispatched 25,000 troops to the Middle East. Operation Granby would eventually find 53,462 UK troops in the Gulf region. These forces were under the command of Air Marshal Andrew Wilson in theatre, headquartered in the Saudi capital of Riyadh, until he was succeeded in October by General Sir Peter de la Billière in October, and finally under the command of

A soldier of the Staffordshire Regiment, 1st Armoured Regiment, participates in exercises in Saudi Arabia. *(US Army via Wikimedia Commons)*

A Syrian Army officer glances sternly at the camera while deployed during Desert Shield. *(US Department of Defense via Wikimedia Commons)*

Air Vice Marshal Ian Macfadyen from March 1991. Only nine days after the Iraqi invasion of Kuwait, the Royal Air Force had reached the Middle East with a dozen Panavia Tornado F3 fighters of No. 5 (AC) Squadron, designated Army Co-operation, and No. 29 (F) Squadron operating out of RAF Coningsby. In the weeks that followed, RAF strength was regularly augmented with additional Tornado fighters bringing the total to 18, and 350 ground support personnel along with 27 flight crews.

On the ground, the initial British Army contribution of the 7th Armoured Brigade, the famed Desert Rats, was followed by the 4th Armoured Brigade, and the two components formed the 1st Armoured Division. At its peak, the ground component of the UK military contingent numbered about 28,000 combat and support troops, with 179 Challenger 1 tanks, 316 Warrior armoured personnel carriers, 79 artillery pieces, and 16 MLRS (Multiple Launch Rocket System).

On November 8, President Bush had energised the military option being constructed with Desert Shield, announcing to the world that the US military commitment to the Middle East would be virtually doubled in size and power,

At the height of Desert Shield, a crew of the Egyptian 3rd Armoured Brigade stands beside its M60 tank. *(US National Archives and Records Administration via Wikimedia Commons)*

with more troops and weapons. The directives issued were a clear signal that Coalition – particularly American – resolve would not waiver as the coming days would constitute an offensive capability, significantly beyond only a defensive bulwark against further aggression.

While the US and the UK took the lead in developing a military presence to counter an Iraqi army of an estimated one million soldiers, Secretaries Baker and Cheney were busy cultivating international support for the Desert Shield buildup. With the weight of the series of UN resolutions behind him, Baker visited nine countries in 11 days during September 1990, asking for material and financial support. The press dubbed the whirlwind tour the 'Tin Cup Trip', and his efforts bore substantial fruit.

Baker's first stop was Saudi Arabia, directly threatened by the recent aggression of Saddam Hussein, and the kingdom committed to Coalition use of bases in the country, its armed forces, and a payment of $15bn to defray the immense cost of the military movement and sustainment. Baker went to see representatives of the recently evacuated

A Syrian soldier occupies a foxhole during Desert Shield exercises. *(US Department of Defense via Wikimedia Commons)*

A column of French trucks and armoured vehicles crosses the desert in Saudi Arabia. *(US Department of Defense via Wikimedia Commons)*

Jet aircraft of France, Qatar, Canada and the United States fly together in a show of Coalition co-operation. *(US Air Force via Wikimedia Commons)*

Kuwaiti government in Taif, Saudi Arabia, where some sources said that the Emir had headquartered in a Sheraton Hotel. Baker requested the same financial contribution from the Kuwaitis and secured their pledge.

President Mubarak of Egypt was notably angered by the actions of Saddam Hussein, who had previously provided assurances that no invasion of Kuwait was planned. Mubarak received Baker warmly, and soon 20,000 Egyptian troops were mobilised. Egypt had been marginalised among Arab nations since the Camp David Accords and peace with Israel in the spring of 1979. However, Mubarak remained a moderate presence in the Middle East, and in his frustration recognised an opportunity to reintegrate more fully with other nations in common opposition to the Iraqi aggression. Further, Egypt received more than $7bn in debt forgiveness from the United States for its participation in Desert Shield.

Baker then travelled to Helsinki, Finland, accompanying President Bush during the crucial summit with Soviet leader Mikhail Gorbachev. He briefed NATO foreign ministers on the current situation in the Middle East and the results of the Helsinki summit on September 10 in Brussels, Belgium, and then flew on to Moscow for further talks with Gorbachev and Soviet Foreign Minister Eduard Shevardnadze, before undertaking one of the most interesting diplomatic exchanges of the period.

President Hafez Assad of Syria was, like Saddam Hussein, a Ba'athist. Assad had come to power in 1971, but despite their common political views, the Syrian leader distrusted Saddam. The US and Syria had been at odds for some time following the unrest in Lebanon and the 1983 terrorist bombing of the US Marine barracks in Beirut, Lebanon, that killed 241 American military personnel and resulted in the severing of direct diplomatic ties between the two countries.

Nevertheless, Baker made a magnanimous overture, flying to Damascus to meet face-to-face with Assad. During their frank discussions, the Syrian leader

Soldiers of the US 325th Airborne Infantry Regiment service a 105mm howitzer. *(US Army via Wikimedia Commons)*

An American and Saudi soldiers train with a Stinger shoulder-fired missile. *(US Army via Wikimedia Commons)*

pledged 100,000 troops to the effort to oust his Ba'athist rival from Kuwait. Such a commitment was central to the alignment of other Arab states in support of Desert Shield, and in exchange for his co-operation Assad was allowed to take further action against opposition to Syrian domination of Lebanon. The Syrians were also promised at least $1bn in weapons shipments – much of these delivered to Syria through other Arab countries in fulfilling the bargain.

Although Iran remained neutral in the Desert Shield/Storm crisis, the country did condemn the Iraqi invasion of Kuwait. To secure that neutrality, Baker was involved in the approval of loans to Iran from the World Bank. The Americans had opposed the World Bank's extension of credit to the Islamic Republic for some time following the seizure of the US Embassy in Tehran by Iranian militants on November 4, 1979, and the subsequent holding of American citizens as hostages for 444 days. However, the non-interference of Iran in the present situation was deemed essential.

By mid-September, Baker was in Rome, where he secured co-operation from the Italian government for the use of bases in the country and received a commitment of supplies and logistics support, and later the deployment of eight Tornado fighter planes and four ships of the Italian Navy to the Persian Gulf.

On the 25th, the Secretary of State was in Bonn, West Germany, meeting with Chancellor Helmut Kohl. Although the post-World War Two constitution of West Germany forbade military involvement outside the borders of

An M-551 Sheridan tank of the US 82nd Airborne Division moves forward during live fire exercises in Saudi Arabia. *(US Government via Wikimedia Commons)*

the country, Kohl pledged $2bn in financial support to the Desert Shield effort along with transportation for Egyptian troops to the Gulf region, and further offered military and economic aid to Turkey, a NATO country and key centre of Coalition operations in the build-up. Japan, also bound by constitutional restrictions on the deployment of troops after World War Two, pledged $6.6bn to Desert Shield.

When the United Nations Security Council passed Resolution 678 approving the use of military force to eject the Iraqis from Kuwait if they did not voluntarily withdraw by January 15, 1991, it was apparent that the

Secretary of State James Baker confers with President George HW Bush in November 1990. *(George HW Bush Presidential Library and Museum via Wikimedia Commons)*

A US soldier directs the crew of an M1A1 Abrams main battle tank arriving for deployment. *(US National Archives and Records Administration via Wikimedia Commons)*

vast majority of the civilised world had been galvanised against Saddam Hussein. When the Security Council vote was taken, only Yemen and Cuba opposed the measure, while the People's Republic of China abstained. The depth and breadth of opposition to Iraq's seizure of Kuwait and its installation of a puppet regime were startling.

Even as the US-led Coalition marshalled its military might in the Middle East, diplomatic efforts were ongoing. However, with each passing day, the hopes for a peaceful solution were diminished. Prior to the approval of Resolution 678, the UN had passed 11 separate resolutions opposing the Iraqi action. Time was running out for Saddam Hussein. ◼

UH-60 Blackhawk helicopters lift 105mm howitzers during Desert Shield manoeuvres. *(Creative Commons US Army Materiel Command via Wikimedia Commons)*

PRESIDENT GEORGE HW BUSH

George HW Bush stood for this presidential portrait in 1989. *(US National Archives and Records Administration via Wikimedia Commons)*

A POLITICAL FIGURE WHOSE breadth of experience led to defining moments in foreign policy during his administration, George HW Bush, 41st President of the United States, was the central figure in the establishment of the Coalition that won the Gulf War and defeated the Iraqi forces of Saddam Hussein.

Bush had previously served two terms as Vice President of the United States under President Ronald Reagan. He was ambassador to the United Nations, Director of the Central Intelligence Agency, chairman of the Republican National Committee, a Congressman representing the 7th District of Texas, and chief of the liaison office to the People's Republic of China prior to winning election to the White House in 1988. Bush led the West during the final years of the Cold War and was in office during the reunification of Germany.

However, among his sternest tests was the confrontation with an aggressive Iraqi nation that invaded Kuwait on August 2, 1990. Bush knew the stakes were high when responding to the crisis, and he was instrumental in building the alliance that eventually resorted to military force to remove the Iraqis from their neighbour's territory. After the invasion, Bush was engaged in months of diplomatic effort to resolve the crisis and persuade the Iraqis to withdraw from Kuwait. Meanwhile, the United Nations Security Council issued a resolution for the peaceful withdrawal, and set January 15, 1991, as the deadline.

Just four days after the invasion, Bush addressed the world and boldly stated: "This aggression will not stand." Afterwards, he managed to galvanise much of the world, including nations as diverse as Arab countries, Russia, the People's Republic of China, and those of Western Europe against Saddam Hussein. The concern not only that Saddam's ambitions extended beyond simply the occupation of Kuwait had stirred other nations of the Middle East, particularly Saudi Arabia, to seek military support. Although a crippling national debt and low oil prices following the Iran-Iraq War of 1980-88 were catalysts that led to Saddam's aggression, there was no doubt that a desire for pre-eminence in the region was a further threat to peace.

President Bush displayed tremendous diplomatic skill during the build-up and execution of Desert Shield and Desert Storm, most notably in persuading Israel to refrain from retaliation when Iraqi Scud missiles were launched against the country. Although the immediate aims of the Coalition military operation were achieved, Bush was criticised in the wake of Desert Storm for allowing Saddam Hussein to remain in power.

Navy pilot George HW Bush is shown in the cockpit of his torpedo bomber during World War Two. *(US Navy via Wikimedia Commons)*

Born into a wealthy and prominent New England family in Milton, Massachusetts, on June 12, 1924, Bush was educated at the prestigious Phillips Academy and Yale University prior to joining the US Naval Reserve, and serving as a pilot in World War Two in the Pacific. He was shot down while flying a torpedo bomber and rescued by a US submarine, receiving the Distinguished Flying Cross for the mission. Altogether he flew 58 combat missions. He married the former Barbara Pierce in 1945, and the couple had six children. Their eldest, George W Bush, was elected 43rd President of the United States in 2001. From that time, his father was often referred to as Bush 41.

The elder Bush served a single term as president, losing in the 1992 election to Democrat Bill Clinton. Despite foreign policy successes, a weak economy and the influence of third-party candidate Ross Perot combined to give Clinton the deciding edge at the polls. Bush was active in his later years and died at the age of 94 on November 30, 2018. ■

President Bush meets with close advisors in the Oval Office as the Persian Gulf crisis deepens. *(US National Archives and Records Administration via Wikimedia Commons)*

PRIME MINISTER MARGARET THATCHER

Displaying her famous steadfast countenance, Prime Minister Thatcher reviews troops in 1990. *(White House Photo Office via Wikimedia Commons)*

"**T**HIS IS NO time to go wobbly!" she advised the American President. Prime Minister Margaret Thatcher, dubbed the Iron Lady by a Soviet reporter, never minced her words. When the time for decisive action occurred in the Persian Gulf, she was steadfast and urged George HW Bush to demonstrate the necessary resolve to drive Saddam Hussein and the Iraqi army from Kuwait. She was firm in her stand that aggression would not prevail.

Even though her term in office was fast drawing to a close, Thatcher was concerned with the future. Domestic issues and fears that she could not generate enough votes among the people to sustain her Conservative Party's leadership role in Britain, she resigned her office in late 1990, giving way to John Major. However, her influence had already charted the course for Britain and the free world in its response to Iraqi brutality.

Thatcher's government authorised the deployment of military forces to the Gulf region in August 1990, the same month that Saddam Hussein's army invaded its neighbour to the south. Although some factions in Parliament criticised her somewhat secretive approach to the crisis in the Middle East, and her strong preference for military action rather than reliance on economic sanctions alone, it must be concluded in the final analysis that her bolstering of Coalition determination was crucial in the victory that was Desert Storm.

Thatcher was born in Grantham, Lincolnshire, on October 13, 1925. She was a graduate of Somerville College, Oxford, and worked as a research chemist before becoming a barrister. She entered politics in the 1950s and was elected to Parliament in 1959. She served as secretary of state for education and science in the administration of Prime Minister Edward Heath, and rose to lead the Conservative Party. She was elected Prime Minister in 1979 after becoming the first woman to head a major political party in the UK. Subsequently, she became the longest serving Prime Minister of Great Britain in the 20th century, 1979 to 1990. During her tenure, the British military launched an arduous but successful operation to eject Argentine military forces from the distant Falkland Islands in the spring of 1982.

Margaret Thatcher survived an assassination attempt by the Irish Republican Army in 1984 and achieved some measure of economic success with the 'Big Bang' of the later 1980s, although her support of the poll tax added to her polarising characteristics within the British electorate. In later years, she was lauded as a prominent political figure, not only in Britain but worldwide.

Thatcher received the Presidential Medal of Freedom from the United States and was elevated to the peerage as Baroness Thatcher following her 1992 retirement from the House of Commons. Her perspective on the Gulf War was prescient, and she commented on the prospects for the future: "The victories of peace will take longer than the battles of war." She died after suffering a stroke on April 8, 2013, at the age of 87. ■

Prime Minister Thatcher receives the Presidential Medal of Freedom in March 1991. *(US National Archives and Records Administration via Wikimedia Commons)*

Prime Minister Margaret Thatcher and President George HW Bush confer during a meeting in August 1990. *(George Bush Presidential Library via Wikimedia Commons)*

PRIME MINISTER JOHN MAJOR

Prime Minister John Major meets with President George HW Bush at Camp David in December 1990. *(George HW Bush Presidential Library and Museum via Wikimedia Commons)*

JOHN MAJOR TOOK office as Prime Minister of Great Britain on November 28, 1990, when the British commitment to Operation Desert Shield/Storm was already fully affirmed. The British military deployment to oust Iraqi forces from Kuwait was second only to that of the United States, and Major stayed the course throughout the campaign.

In one of the first significant tests of his administration's foreign policy, Major worked closely with President George HW Bush and other international leaders as a key player in the Coalition, which included 39 countries that contributed in some form. Although the decision to participate had been made, the Prime Minister was responsible for the final arrangements of the commitment, and kept the House of Commons informed on the progress.

On January 8, 1991, in the days leading up to the inception of the armed conflict, Major visited British troops at their bases in Saudi Arabia and bolstered their morale. When the war was over, he returned to the Persian Gulf region and congratulated the troops, telling them: "You'll be home soon."

Nevertheless, Major did not take the responsibility for Britain's deployment lightly. When questioned about his perspective on the coming war, he thoughtfully conveyed concerns. "Your whole focus is on it," he commented. "You don't suddenly have a meeting for an hour on Tuesday morning and then go away and forget it, despite other issues. It is actually on your mind every waking moment, and sometimes when you are asleep as well, frankly."

Major was born in London on March 29, 1943. Unlike most other successful participants in the political arena, he did not pursue as college degree and left secondary school at the age of 16. After working as a bank accountant for some time, he entered the political arena but failed to win election to Parliament twice in 1974. He rode the coattails of a Conservative landslide to a seat in the House of Commons in 1979 and rose steadily within the party ranks, with his own political acumen and the patronage of prominent members, including Thatcher.

He became chief secretary to the Treasury in 1987 and foreign secretary in the summer of 1979. Three months later, he was elevated to Chancellor of the Exchequer and became prominent among the leaders of the Conservative Party. When Thatcher contemplated her own resignation, she threw support to Major for the office of Prime Minister, and he subsequently triumphed in a three-way contest. After winning the general election of 1992 decisively, Major was confronted with persistent economic recession, but also succeeded in obtaining a temporary ceasefire in the conflict in Northern Ireland.

Economic pressures, political scandal, and the misgivings over monetary policy involving the Exchange Rate Mechanism led to the end of 18 years of Conservative majority government in 1997, when the Labour Party and Tony Blair won decisively in the general elections.

Major had been a stabilising figure during the days of the Gulf War and once offered: "I think I was up every night 'til two, three o'clock in the morning to see how it was going and then back up awake again at six o'clock to see how it had gone… I think we are very conscious that older men and women send younger men and women to war." ∎

John Major held the office of British Prime Minister during Operation Desert Storm. *(US Government via Wikimedia Commons)*

Prime Minister John Major poses during a meeting with Cabinet members at 10 Downing Street. *(UK Government via Wikimedia Commons)*

SADDAM HUSSEIN

THE CURTAIN FELL on his ambitious but odious life on December 30, 2006. Saddam Hussein, captured three years earlier during the war that toppled his oppressive regime in Iraq, was tried and convicted of crimes against humanity, and found justice at the end of a rope.

The ruler of Ba'athist Iraq had remained in power for 12 years after leading his country into the disaster of the 1990-91 Persian Gulf War. Coalition forces had crushed his military, ejecting its remnants from neighbouring Kuwait, but allowing the ruthless despot to remain in power. Perhaps the grand strategy that left Saddam Hussein at the head of the repressive regime then was simply a case of the devil that was known rather than further destabilisation in the region that might allow militant Islamic factions loyal to Iran to gain a wider foothold in the troubled Middle East.

However, since the end of the Gulf War, the Iraqi leader had flouted the terms of the Gulf War peace, failing to co-operate with United Nations teams sent to inspect facilities for the storage and production of weapons of mass destruction. In order to contain the Iraqis, a no-fly zone had been imposed along with trade sanctions, and submission to the UN inspections to enforce prohibition of nuclear, chemical, and biological weapons. Iraq was also suspected as a potential state sponsor of terror.

Despite these terms intended to keep the dictator in a box, Saddam authorised the use of chemical weapons against his own people, wreaking vengeance and killing scores of Kurdish civilians and rival Shi'ite Muslims suspected of disloyally co-operating with the Coalition during the Gulf War or with Iran during the 1980-88 war with that country, and plotting rebellion. He had been known to perpetrate such crimes in the early years of his rule, and it was a single such incident, the killing of 148 Iraqi Shi'ite Muslims in the town of Dujail in 1982, that ultimately sent him to the gallows. He was known to have used chemical weapons against the Kurds on more than one occasion, particularly the murder of up to 5,000 people in the town of Halabja in 1988.

Saddam Hussein was born a Sunni Muslim near the city of Tikrit on April 28, 1937, and was sent to live with an uncle in Baghdad. He father died before he was born, and his mother wanted nothing to do with the boy. He joined the Ba'ath Party in 1957 and participated in the attempted assassination of Iraqi Prime Minister Abd al-Karim Qasim. He escaped to Syria and Egypt, recovering from wounds received during the attempt. After returning to Iraq, he was jailed along with other Ba'athists and escaped after several years in custody to become a principal plotter in the coup d'etat that placed the Ba'ath Party in power.

Assuming the presidency of Iraq in 1979, Saddam ruled with a cabal that espoused a curious amalgam of Iraqi nationalism and socialism. Bent on extending Iraqi influence,

On trial for his life, Saddam Hussein speaks in his own defence during courtroom proceedings. *(US Department of Defense via Wikimedia Commons)*

possibly even achieving hegemony in the Middle East, he embarked on the costly war with Iran that ended in cease-fire after both nations had absorbed tremendous casualties and economic hardship.

Saddam continued to build up his military, however, and the August 1990 invasion of Kuwait was initiated as he sought to exploit that oil-rich country's wealth for his own aggressive enterprise, and the rehabilitation of Iraq's failing economy. After his defeat at the hands of the Coalition, he brutally suppressed Shi'ite and Kurdish uprisings within the country. But his recalcitrance proved his undoing. During the brief war of 2003, he was captured in the town of Ad-Dawr, pulled from a 'spider hole', along with a Glock pistol and cache of $750,000 US dollars.

He uttered: "I am Saddam Hussein. I am the president of Iraq, and I am willing to negotiate." However, such a time had passed, and he was made to pay for his transgressions. ∎

Saddam Hussein meets with the Prime Minister of Kuwait in 1990, weeks before his army invaded the neighbouring country. *(Public Domain Iraqi News Agency via Wikimedia Commons)*

This grainy image of Saddam Hussein was taken from a broadcast as he spoke during a 1979 purge of the Ba'ath Party. *(Public Domain photographer unknown via Wikimedia Commons)*

GENERAL NORMAN
SCHWARZKOPF

General Norman Schwarzkopf ended his military career after leading Coalition forces to victory in the Gulf War.
(US Army via Wikimedia Commons)

THE MOST IMPOSING and iconic military figure to emerge from the Gulf War was Herbert Norman Schwarzkopf, a four-star general of the US Army who had served for 35 years, taken charge of United States Central Command (CENTCOM) in 1988, and in turn assumed responsibility for the Coalition armed forces that ejected the occupying Iraqis from Kuwait.

Schwarzkopf was highly intelligent with an IQ of 168. Beyond that, he proved himself not only a master of coalition warfare, but also an adroit spokesman who managed the media with incredible skill. Schwarzkopf carried out daily press briefings punctuated with startling video footage depicting the destruction and degradation of enemy military with a common-sense delivery in response to questions from the reporters.

A 1956 graduate of the US Military Academy at West Point, standing 43rd in a class of 480, Schwarzkopf also earned a Master's degree in mechanical and aerospace engineering from the University of Southern California. Born into a military family in Trenton, New Jersey, on August 22, 1934, he was the son of Brigadier General Norman Schwarzkopf, Sr, a 1917 West Point graduate. The boy attended Bordentown Military Institute near Trenton, but the military life required relocation on several occasions. During his formative years, Schwarzkopf lived in Iran from 1946, gaining some insight into Middle Eastern culture, then moving to Geneva, Switzerland, and again to

Iran by 1951. He completed secondary school at Valley Forge Military Academy in Pennsylvania.

Impressive physically, Norman Schwarzkopf stood 6ft 3in tall and weighed 240lb. He played football, wrestled, and sang in the chapel choir at West Point, sometimes directing the choral group. On the edge of the Vietnam era,

he served as a platoon leader and company executive officer with the 101st Airborne Division and with the 6th Infantry Division in Berlin, Germany, staring across the dividing line and the Berlin Wall at the Soviet military presence, his training had been designed to defeat in the event of war with the communists.

General Schwarzkopf sits behind President George HW Bush in a Humvee in Saudi Arabia.
(US National Archives and Records Administration via Wikimedia Commons)

General Norman Schwarzkopf assumes command at CENTCOM in November 1988.
(US Army via Wikimedia Commons)

Then-Colonel Norman Schwarzkopf confers with other officers during exercises in California in 1977. *(Creative Commons Gen Rees 1977 via Wikimedia Commons)*

After the Iraqi invasion of Kuwait, Schwarzkopf took command in Operation Desert Shield, the buildup of Coalition forces in the autumn and winter of 1990. He worked closely with Secretary of Defense Dick Cheney and General Colin Powell, then Chairman of the Joint Chiefs of Staff. He strove to gain the trust of Arab regimes in the region, particularly that of King Fahd of Saudi Arabia as Coalition forces were obliged to use bases in the country as staging areas for the coming offensive of Desert Storm. Schwarzkopf also worked closely with capable lieutenants such as Army Generals William Pagonis and Calvin Waller, and Air Force General Charles Horner. His command co-operation with General Peter de la Billière, leader of British forces, and General Michel Roquejeoffre, chief of the French military contingent, was essential to the ultimate victory.

Schwarzkopf led the effort to develop the winning strategy that shattered the Iraqi military in the 100-hour ground war. Some sources attribute his strategic and tactical success to following the lessons of Field Marshal Bernard Montgomery in the epic Battle of El Alamein during World War Two.

After the Gulf War, Schwarzkopf returned to the United States and received widespread acclaim. He was honoured with a parade down Broadway in New York, awarded the Presidential Medal of Freedom, and was knighted by Queen Elizabeth II. He declined invitations to head the Joint Chiefs of Staff or to run for political office, choosing retirement in August 1991. From there, he devoted his energy to the recovery of the grizzly bear from the endangered species list and briefly worked as an analyst for NBC News. He demonstrated proficiency as a public speaker and served numerous charities, several of them related to children. He wrote a memoir titled *It Doesn't Take a Hero* and expressed concerns over the US-led invasion of Iraq in 2003, worrying that American reserve troops had not received sufficient training prior to deployment.

Schwarzkopf died in Tampa on December 27, 2012, aged 78. He is remembered today for his leadership, straightforward approach to every facet of his professional experience, and skilled management of the greatest military endeavour since World War Two. Norman Schwarzkopf stands perhaps tallest among all military commanders of the latter half of the 20th century. ■

Standing in the shadow of a statue of General Douglas MacArthur, General Norman Schwarzkopf speaks at West Point. *(Creative Commons Dale Cruse via Wikimedia Commons)*

As American involvement in Vietnam increased, Schwarzkopf felt compelled to volunteer for combat duty. He was "in country" by 1965 and experienced combat for the first time at Pleiku in Vietnam, while serving as an advisor to South Vietnamese airborne troops. He completed two tours of duty in Vietnam – in between finishing a stint as an instructor at West Point and marrying Brenda Holsinger, a TWA flight attendant, in 1968. Even then, Lieutenant Colonel Schwarzkopf was outspoken. While leading a battalion of the 198th Infantry Brigade, he successfully raised unit morale and eradicated drug use, disillusionment, and discipline issues.

At the same time, Schwarzkopf called rear areas of the US military presence in Southeast Asia "cesspools" of staff and command incompetence. He preferred the front lines and gained a reputation as an officer who fought beside his men rather than directing operations from a bunker safely distanced. After various post-Vietnam command roles and surgery for back problems probably caused by parachute jumps, Schwarzkopf participated in active operations in the Caribbean island of Grenada in 1983. He served as deputy commander of US forces committed to protecting Americans during a pro-Marxist coup, and the restoration of lawful government there.

Further senior staff appointments led to CENTCOM, headquartered at MacDill Air Force Base in Tampa, Florida, in 1988. Commanding 200,000 service personnel in 19 countries, Schwarzkopf focused on the threat of Soviet incursions into the Middle East following the Red Army advance into Afghanistan. Despotism had already emerged with Saddam Hussein and the Ba'ath Party in Iraq, and the hostage crisis in Iran as Islamic fundamentalists seized the US Embassy in Tehran, deposing the Shah and the royal family nearly a decade earlier. The Iran-Iraq War erupted in 1988, prompting further emphasis on combat preparedness in the region. And by the late 1980s, even as the threat from expansionist communism decreased with the Soviet Union teetering on the brink of collapse, concerns remained.

General Schwarzkopf and General Colin Powell confer during a Gulf War press conference, 1991. *(US Army via Wikimedia Commons)*

M1A1 ABRAMS
MAIN BATTLE TANK

DURING THE GULF War, the superiority of the M1A1 Abrams main battle tank over the Soviet-era T-72 and others was starkly demonstrated. The battlefield was the ultimate proving ground of a combat system's worth, and the M1A1, named after famed US Army General Creighton Abrams, came through in exemplary fashion.

Although 14 Abrams tanks were damaged and nine lost during Desert Storm operations, none of these were the result of enemy fire. Seven of those destroyed fell to friendly fire, and two others were intentionally destroyed to prevent their capture by hostile forces. In sharp contrast, the Abrams was clearly dominant, with 1,848 M1A1s deployed to Saudi Arabia, and these in turn accounting for an estimated 3,300 enemy T-72, T-62, and T-54/55 tanks.

In tank versus tank combat, the Abrams, manned by highly trained crews, performed admirably at the Battle of 73 Easting, Objective Norfolk, and elsewhere. To date, the Abrams combat system has been purchased by at least ten other countries.

The origin of the M1 Abrams lay in the failure of a joint venture between the United States and the Federal Republic of Germany to develop a third-generation main battle tank

The M1A1 Abrams main battle tank proved itself a lethal combat system during the Gulf War. *(US Air Force via Wikimedia Commons)*

in the 1970s. The enterprise's demise led to the design of two iconic tanks, the Abrams and the German Leopard 2. The first XM-1 prototype underwent field evaluation in 1976. Two years later, Chrysler Corporation began production, and in 1980 the first operational M1 was delivered to the US Army.

Although some examples of the M1 were deployed to the Middle East during the Gulf War, the majority of US main battle tanks were of the M1A1 configuration, which emerged in 1985. The M1A1 incorporated several upgrades from the original tank, including the introduction of a 120mm Rheinmetall L44 (M256) smoothbore gun, replacing the original British-designed 105mm rifled main armament. The M1A1 also deployed, with improvements to the NBC (nuclear, biological, chemical) defence system, and improved armour protection based on the original Chobham, and including plates of depleted uranium equivalent to 38ins of rolled homogeneous steel. Blast doors were added to the engine compartment, while the suspension, transmission and drives were improved, along with other enhancements.

Powered by the Honeywell AGT 1500 gas turbine engine designed by Lycoming Textron, the M1A1 was capable of a top speed in excess of 42mph. Secondary armament included a pair of M240 7.62mm machine guns, one mounted coaxially with the main gun and the other mounted for the loader. The commander accessed a single 12.7mm (.50-calibre) machine gun from the turret. The M1A1 crew of four consisted of a commander, driver, loader, and gunner.

Enhancement programs are expected to extend the service life of the Abrams tank series into the mid-21st century, and to date at least 10,000 have been manufactured. ■

An M1A1 Abrams main battle tank is shown during exercises in the Kuwaiti desert. *(US Department of Defense via Wikimedia Commons)*

An M1A1 Abrams tank of the US Marine Corps fires its main 120mm smoothbore weapon. *(US Navy via Wikimedia Commons)*

A stream of 25mm shells exits the barrel of the M242 chain gun of a Bradley fighting vehicle. *(U.S. Army via Wikimedia Commons)*

M2/M3 BRADLEY FIGHTING VEHICLE

WHEN THE M2/M3 Bradley fighting vehicle entered service with the US military in 1981, it had already weathered the storm of viability in the halls of the American Congress due to cost overruns amid a wave of defence spending cuts in the post-Vietnam era. However, it had been recognised that a replacement for the venerable M113 armoured personnel carrier was necessary.

The Bradley, named after famed US Army General Omar N Bradley, was designed to transport combat-ready infantrymen into battle while also providing close fire support. It was developed in two quite similar variants, the M2 Infantry and M3 Cavalry. The M2 was to carry a crew of three, along with seven combat soldiers and that number was later reduced to six troops who accessed the internal compartment via hatches or a rear ramp. The M3 variant carried two scout infantrymen along with improved communications equipment to allow the Bradley to serve in the reconnaissance or command role. The single major design difference between the two is the absence of firing slits in the M3 rear compartment.

Powered by a 500hp, eight-cylinder supercharged diesel engine, and in 1991 an upgraded 600hp Cummins VTA903T diesel, the M2/M3 was capable of a top speed of 41mph. Its combination of speed and firepower were effectively demonstrated during the Gulf War. The service record of the Bradley provided an effective response to its detractors as the vehicle became essential in the fighting at the Battle of 73 Easting and elsewhere. In fact, some sources credit the Bradley with the destruction of more Iraqi tanks than the M1A1 Abrams main battle tank.

The Bradley and its crew of three are protected by aluminium alloy explosive reactive armour, while the main armament consists of the 25mm McDonnell Douglas M242 Bushmaster chain gun, a highly effective automatic cannon, and the TOW anti-tank missile package. The integrated sight unit is housed within the T-BAT-II (TOW-Bushmaster Armoured Turret-Two Man). The Bushmaster fires high-explosive or armour piercing ammunition at a rate of up to 200 rounds per minute. The TOW or TOW II anti-tank missile, developed by Hughes Aircraft, was capable of defeating any Iraqi tank and fired from a tube launcher adjacent to the turret. A secondary 7.62mm M240C machine gun is mounted coaxially in the turret.

During the Gulf War, a total of 2,200 M2/M3 Bradley fighting vehicles were deployed to the Middle East. Only 20 were lost, and 17 of these were attributed to incidents of friendly fire. Twelve more were damaged. From 1980 to 1995, nearly 7,000 examples were produced. ■

This M2 Bradley Infantry Fighting Vehicle is shown on display at Fort Irwin, California. *(US Army via Wikimedia Commons)*

US soldiers enter an M2 Bradley Infantry Fighting Vehicle via the rear ramp. *(US Air Force via Wikimedia Commons)*

CHALLENGER 1
MAIN BATTLE TANK

An Iraqi tank erupts in a fireball after a hit from the 120mm gun aboard a Challenger 1. *(US Department of Defense via Wikimedia Commons)*

RONICALLY, THE DEVELOPMENT of the British Challenger 1 main battle tank, considered the bridge between the older Chieftain and the Challenger 2, which is the primary such weapon of the UK forces in the 21st century, has its roots in the Middle East.

The Challenger 1, known only as Challenger until the introduction of its successor, was derived from the Shir II, a radical modification of the Chieftain intended for sale to Iran. However, when the Shah was toppled in 1979, the order for 1,225 Shir II tanks was abruptly cancelled. At the same time, a joint venture between Britain and the Federal Republic of Germany, intended to produce a more standardised NATO table of organisation and equipment, fell apart. The British then initiated their MTB-80 program, but this also foundered amid cost overruns and the swift advance of technology.

The alternative was the reinvention of the Shir II, from the start considered a temporary solution to the British tank dilemma. All acknowledged that the solution was short term, but it proved to bring about the Challenger, which will forever be linked to the Gulf War as the main firepower fist of the UK 1st Armoured Division and the destroyer of approximately 300 Iraqi tanks. In the easternmost van of the Coalition VII Corps, the division blasted the enemy 46th Mechanised Brigade, 52nd Armoured Brigade, and much of three Iraqi infantry divisions. Approximately 221 of the tanks were deployed during Desert Storm and none were lost or damaged. Only 420 Challenger 1 tanks were completed by the Royal Ordnance Factory between 1983, the year the tank entered service, and 1990.

The Challenger 1 was powered by a 1,200hp Perkins Engine Company Condor V-12 diesel engine that produced a top speed of 36mph. It was the first tank to employ revolutionary composite Chobham armour. With its crew of four, the tank was laid out in standard British design with the engine to the rear, fighting compartment in the centre, and driving compartment forward, where the driver's seat reclined to reduce the profile of the vehicle to less than 9½ft. The main Challenger weapon was the proven Royal Ordnance L11A5 120mm rifled gun, while secondary 7.62mm L8A2 and L37A2 machine guns were mounted in the turret, one slaved coaxially with the main weapon and the other positioned by the commander's cupola.

Although the Challenger 1 was considered by many experts to be a vast improvement over the Chieftain, mechanical issues persisted after it was accepted by the British Army, including problems with laser sighting equipment, engine generator drive, and gearbox functionality. As the new Challenger 2 came on line in 1998, many Challenger 1 tanks were subsequently transferred to the Jordanian Army. ■

This Challenger 1 was photographed in 2009 at the Tank Museum, Bovington. *(Creative Commons Simon Q via Wikimedia Commons)*

A Challenger 1 main battle tank of the Royal Scots Dragoon Guards near Kuwait City during the Gulf War. *(US Department of Defense via Wikimedia Commons)*

This Iraqi T-72 main battle tank was neutralised in its dug-in desert position as the ground phase of the Gulf War proceeded. *(US Marine Corps via Wikimedia Commons)*

T-72 MAIN BATTLE TANK

WHEN THE GULF War was over, the blackened hulks of hundreds of Iraqi tanks were strewn across the deserts of their home country and neighbouring Kuwait. A number of these were the ubiquitous T-72, nicknamed Ural, designed and built in the Soviet Union, and in several client states under licence during the 1970s. The T-72 remains one of the most numerous tanks in the world today, even after its dismal showing in the 1990-91 conflict.

However, at the heart of that desert debacle lay the simple fact that the Iraqis deployed T-72s that were inferior to Coalition armoured vehicles because their technology had rarely, if ever, been upgraded to current fighting standards after they were acquired. The T-72s deployed by the Republican Guard and other Iraqi divisions fought from a disadvantaged perspective, often with equipment and systems aboard that were at least a generation behind that of their adversaries. Crew training, and the resolve of many of the Iraqi soldiers who opposed the Coalition, no doubt also played a role in the decimation of the Ural and other tanks deployed by the Iraqi army.

Introduced in 1973, the T-72 was a concurrent tank design that resulted from a competition between the Morozov KB project in Kharkov and the Uralvagon KB project under the leadership of Leonard Kartsev in Nizhny Tagil. The goal was to produce a main battle tank for the export market and for some echelons of the Soviet Red Army and client states of the Warsaw Pact. The T-72 was developed in tandem with the T-64, which was intended for frontline Red Army armoured units that faced NATO forces in Europe. The T-72 was, therefore, a less expensive alternative to wholesale production of the T-64,

and offered an entrée for Soviet armour into the lucrative world arms export market. In short, the T-72 was a compromise in cost, firepower, and technology that has survived more than a half century in service with many countries.

The Iraqi T-72s were most commonly the M1 variant, nicknamed 'Lion of Babylon', and these were not well maintained and particularly lacked the latest in technology, while also suffering from lack of maintenance and worn-out barrels in their main armament. They were estimated to have been about 20 years behind the state-of-the-art Coalition tanks they faced in combat readiness.

Nevertheless, the T-72 in its best shape was and is a formidable weapon. Its main armament consists of the 125mm smoothbore 2A46M cannon, which outgunned NATO tanks when first introduced in the early 1970s. Secondary armament consists of a pintle-mounted 12.7mm machine gun above the commander's hatch and a 7.62mm coaxial machine gun in

the turret. Its 780hp, 12-cylinder, W-46 diesel engine was superb when well maintained and produced a top speed of about 37mph. The turret was typical of Soviet designs, resembling a frying pan with its elliptical shape that tends to give the tank a characteristic forward-leaning profile. An automatic loader eliminated the need for a fourth crewman, and the interior was typical of Soviet-era tank construction, which sacrificed crew comfort for reduced production time and expense, and enhanced speed and manoeuvrability.

During the Gulf War, T-72 losses are estimated to have topped 100 vehicles, a fraction of the total Iraqi armour losses, which included the T-62 and T-54/55, along with Chinese-made T-59 and T-69 tanks that were essentially copies of Soviet designs. ∎

This Iraqi T-72 main battle tank was destroyed in combat by Coalition forces during the 100-hour ground war. *(US Army via Wikimedia Commons)*

This T-72M main battle tank is similar to those deployed by the Iraqi military during the Gulf War. *(Creative Commons Adam Hauner via Wikimedia Commons)*

T-62 & T-54/55 TANKS

IN THE BURGEONING years of the Cold War, the Soviet Union sought to modernise its armoured forces with an improvement to the legendary T-34/85 medium tank of World War Two fame. The early T-44 effort was unsuccessful; therefore, the new T-54/55 became the first Soviet design of the Cold War era to enter service with the Red Army and to make substantial inroads into the export market, along with the forces of Soviet satellite states.

The T-54 was eventually produced in greater numbers than any other tank in modern history, with an estimated 80,000 or more built between 1948 and the end of production in the early 1980s. The T-54 was similar in appearance to earlier Soviet tanks with an effective main gun, the rifled 100mm D10T. Its Type V-54 V-12 diesel engine was capable of a top speed of 30mph, while the tank was lighter than its NATO contemporaries at just under 40 tons. The T-54 introduced a sleek dome-shaped turret and other characteristics that defined Soviet armoured vehicles of the era, yet there was no consideration for crew comfort or functionality.

The interior of the T-54 was dysfunctional given that three crewmen, commander, gunner, and loader, were all situated on the left side of the turret and therefore vulnerable to being incapacitated by a single hit. Further, the loader was required to perform a series of steps to complete his task in combat, rendering firing inefficient. Although the T-54 did incorporate a number of upgrades, it was continually modified, so much so that in 1958 the latest variant was given its own designation, the T-55. The newer version did eliminate some of the shortcomings in the T-54, particularly the installation of a turret basket, better armour protection, and improved fire control. Since its inception, although outmoded, the T-54/55 has remained a common component of armed forces around the world. The destruction of well over 100 of these in Iraqi service was documented with photographs during the Gulf War.

By the late 1950s, the Soviets embarked on another improvement program based on the T-54/55 design. The T-62 entered service in the summer of 1961 but was not revealed to the public until four years later. It was recognisable not only as a stretched version of the T-55 with its characteristic oval-shaped turret, but also with the improved 115mm smoothbore U-5TS main cannon, which sported an appreciably longer barrel than its D10T predecessor. Notably, the top-loading breech of the weapon made servicing cumbersome and reduced the rate of fire to four rounds per minute. Further, the 115mm cannon could not be loaded while the turret was being traversed. True to form, the interior of the T-62 remained cramped, leading some critics to refer to the layout as an "ergonomic slum".

Overall, the T-62 was considered marginally inferior to contemporary NATO Cold War tanks, retaining many of the attributes of the T-54/55. During the Gulf War, at least 34 examples of the T-62 were destroyed in combat, along with some Chinese-built T-69s, copies of the T-62 manufactured after one was captured by the People's Liberation Army during a border clash with Red Army forces in the late 1960s. ■

Captured during the Gulf War, this Iraqi T-54/55 is on display in the United States. *(US Air Force via Wikimedia Commons)*

An abandoned Iraqi T-62 tank sits amid other military vehicles along the route known as the Highway of Death. *(US Marine Corps via Wikimedia Commons)*

This close-up of the T-54 turret reveals its characteristic oval shape. *(Creative Commons Mohit S via Wikimedia Commons)*

F-15 EAGLE

THE MCDONNELL DOUGLAS F-15 Eagle entered service with the US Air Force (USAF) in 1976 and has shown remarkable longevity over the last half century. To date, it has seen no confirmed losses in air-to-air combat and recorded more than 100 victories in troubled skies. Most of these aerial kills have been achieved by the Israeli Air Force during multiple conflicts.

However, the shining moment for the F-15 occurred during the Gulf War as two of its variants, the F-15C air superiority fighter and the F-15E Strike Eagle air-to-ground support configuration, were workhorses throughout the air and ground components of Operation Desert Shield/Storm.

The F-15C is a single-seat interceptor designed to control the airspace in any theatre of operations, taking on contemporary fighters that were commonly of Soviet design, including the MiG-21, MiG-23, MiG-25, and MiG-29. Along with these, the Iraqi Air Force employed a number of the French-built Mirage F1 aircraft. The F-15 C proved adept at its role while utilising an array of state-of-the-art technology. Its AN/APG-63 Doppler pulse radar allowed recognition and engagement of enemy aircraft at exceptional range, while its assortment of ordnance, including the AIM-7 Sparrow and AIM-9 Sidewinder air-to-air missiles, and the M61 20mm Vulcan cannon, were highly effective.

The F-15C performed several critical missions during the Gulf War such as combat air patrol, escorting strike aircraft, and engaging Iraqi warplanes wherever they were detected. During the war, the F-15 was also operated by the Royal Saudi Air Force and recorded 36 aerial

victories without a single combat loss. Total air superiority was achieved in abut 72 hours.

The two-seat F-15E Strike Eagle was deployed effectively to reduce identified ground targets while retaining its dogfighting capability. The Strike Eagle utilised high resolution ground mapping to detect fixed targets, as well as the AN/APG-70 radar system. Low Altitude Navigation and Targeting Infrared for Night (LANTIRN) allowed the F-15E to operate around the clock. Armament included laser-guided bombs, AGM-65 Maverick, AIM-7 Sparrow, and AIM-9 Sidewinder missiles, the 20mm Vulcan cannon, and standard bombs such as the 2,000-pound Mk 84.

During Desert Storm, the F-15E took out enemy command and control centres, transportation infrastructure, fixed and mobile Scud missile launch sites, and installations deep inside Iraq. The extremely hazardous missions of the Strike Eagle were inherently risky, but only two F-15E aircraft were shot down during the conflict in which the type logged hundreds of sorties.

The F-15 remains in service today. Its powerplant consists of a pair of Pratt & Whitney F100-PW-220 turbofan engines rendering a top speed of Mach 1.2 or 921mph. Its weapons complement is affixed to nine hard points on the wings, fuselage, and a centreline pylon. ■

An F-15C fires an AIM-7 Sparrow missile during exercises. *(US Air Force via Wikimedia Commons)*

An F-15 Eagle of the Royal Saudi Air Force refuels in the air during Operation Desert Shield. *(US Department of Defense via Wikimedia Commons)*

An F-15E Strike Eagle, its weapons package visible, streaks across the sky in the Middle East. *(US Air Force via Wikimedia Commons)*

A USAF F-16 fighter is refuelled from a KC-135 Stratotanker during Gulf War air operations. *(US Air Force via Wikimedia Commons)*

F-16 FIGHTING FALCON

THE F-16 FIGHTING Falcon, or simply Falcon, was developed in the early 1970s following the identification of a need for a new air superiority fighter after the US experience in Vietnam. First developed by General Dynamics in 1974, the single-seat F-16 has exhibited versatility as a multi-role fighter, capable of dogfighting and ground attack support.

During Operation Desert Storm, a total of 251 USAF F-16s were deployed to the Middle East, while the Fighting Falcon was also a mainstay of several other Coalition air forces. The aircraft was regularly utilised in the suppression of Iraqi air defences and in tactical ground support. F-16 pilots also flew combat air patrols during the Desert Shield buildup. F-16s executed the largest single Coalition air raid of the Gulf War on January 19, 1991, attacking a large Iraqi nuclear facility near the capital city of Baghdad. Fifty-six Fighting Falcons participated in the operation. The first combat experience involving the F-16 was in Israeli service over the Beqaa Valley against Syrian forces in the spring of 1981, and the fighter's reputation for effectiveness widened after its use in the Israeli bombing of the Iraqi nuclear facility at Osirak in the same year.

The supersonic F-16 was initially powered by a single General Electric F110-GE-100 turbofan engine with afterburners, or the Pratt and Whitney F100-PW-220 turbofan delivering a top speed in excess of Mach 2 or 1,353mph. Armament included a single M61A1 Vulcan 20mm cannon and various configurations of the AIM-9 Sidewinder air-to-air missile, the 500lb GBU-12 laser-guided bomb, 200lb GBU-10 laser-guided bomb, CBU 89 anti-personnel cluster bombs, CBU-52 anti-armour cluster

An F-16 Fighting Falcon wings its way over the Nevada desert during air exercises. *(US Air Force via Wikimedia Commons)*

An F-16 Fighting Falcon of the South Carolina Air National Guard displays air-to-air missiles among its array of armament. *(US Air Force via Wikimedia Commons)*

bombs, the 500lb MK-82 general purpose bomb, and the 2,000lb MK-84 general purpose bomb. Munitions were affixed to nine hard points; two on the wing tips, one under the fuselage, and six beneath the wings.

In action during the Gulf War, F-16 pilots flew 13,340 combat sorties. Seven Falcons were lost, five due to enemy action and three of these confirmed to Iraqi surface-to-air missiles such as the SA-3, SA-6, and SA-16. One F-16 was damaged by an enemy missile, but the pilot managed to fly 150 miles, returning to friendly territory before ejecting as the engine ceased to function. Two F-16 pilots were captured and held as prisoners until the end of the war. One F-16 was destroyed and its pilot tragically killed during a training accident prior to the inception of the Gulf War air campaign. ■

F/A-18 HORNET

AFTER MAKING ITS combat debut in 1986 operations against the regime of Libyan strongman Muammar Khadafi, the McDonnell Douglas F/A-18 Hornet again proved its worth in the skies above the Middle East during Operation Desert Storm.

In replacing the ageing, A-7 Corsair and F-4 Phantom fighters of the US Navy and Marine Corps, the F/A-18 entered service in 1983 as the first operational all-weather, multi-role fighter of the US military. The aircraft was designed as a ground attack and strike fighter while retaining its capability to dogfight enemy planes to achieve air superiority.

The F/A-18 gave rise to its successor, the Super Hornet, which replaced the Grumman F-14 Tomcat as a frontline Navy fighter and led to the retirement of the original Hornet aircraft from American service in 2019. In the meantime, however, the F/A-18 confirmed its anticipated capabilities in combat. Powered by two F-404-GE-402 enhanced performance turbofan engines, it was capable of a top speed in excess of Mach 1.7, nearly 1,305mph. Its armament included a suite of AIM-7 Sparrow and AIM-9 Sidewinder air-to-air missiles, Maverick air-to-ground missiles, other smart weapons, and the reliable M61A1/A2 Vulcan 20mm cannon. Its Joint Direct Attack Munitions (JDAM) and Joint Stand-Off Weapons (JSOW) were among the premiere weapons in the American arsenal.

During the Gulf War, the F/A-18 was deployed by both the US Navy and Marine Corps in

An F/A-18 Hornet fighter prepares to refuel in the air above the Iraqi desert. *(US Air Force via Wikimedia Commons)*

a combined strength of 190 aircraft. The Hornet flew 4,551 combat sorties and three were lost with seven others damaged. In the opening hours of the conflict, F/A-18 pilots were credited with destroying two Iraqi MiG-21 fighters in air-to-air combat. Both were downed by Sidewinder and Sparrow missiles by pilots flying from the aircraft carrier USS *Saratoga*. The targets were acquired after early warning communications from an E2-C Hawkeye aircraft, and dispatched in just 40 seconds.

The first American combat casualty of the Gulf War was 33-year-old Lieutenant Commander Michael Scott Speicher, whose Hornet was apparently shot down by an air-to-air missile fired from an Iraqi MiG-25 fighter on January 17, 1991. Another F/-18 pilot, Lieutenant Robert Dwyer, was presumed killed in action when his plane was lost over the Persian Gulf in February. Through the course of the conflict, the Hornet rendered excellent service in completing hazardous tactical support missions. One F/A-18 was damaged in both engines by enemy fire, but the pilot managed to fly the crippled plane 125 miles back to base. Within days, the damaged Hornet was repaired and back in service. ◼

An F/A-18 Hornet of the US Navy flies in Middle Eastern skies. *(US Navy via Wikimedia Commons)*

US Marine Corps F/A-18 Hornet fighters taxi on a runway at their base in Bahrain prior to take off in support of Desert Storm. *(US Marine Corps via Wikimedia Commons)*

PANAVIA TORNADO

A total of six RAF Tornados were lost during the Gulf War, three of these prior to the unleashing of the sustained air campaign, and the Italian Air Force lost a single plane. Flying from airfields in Saudi Arabia and Bahrain, the Tornado executed missions with conventional 1,000lb bombs as well as the Low-Altitude Airfield Attack System (LAAAS), also known as JP233, designed to crater enemy runways and render them unusable to Iraqi aircraft. The first Tornado to fall in action during the Gulf War was downed by an Iraqi SA-16 surface-to-air missile during a low altitude bombing run on January 17, 1991, and the second was shot down two days later during a heavy raid on the Iraqi Air Force base at Tallil, near the city of Nasiriyah. During the course of the war, seven airmen of the RAF or the Italian Air Force were captured and held temporarily as prisoners of war. Sources reveal that 12 Tornado airmen were killed in action and three wounded.

The supersonic Tornado is capable of speeds exceeding Mach 2, more than 1,500mph, powered by a pair of Turbo-Union RB199-34R Mk 103 turbofan engines with afterburners. Along with the JP233 and conventional bombs, armament included a single Mauser 27mm internally mounted cannon, AIM-9 Sidewinder air-to-air missiles and other ordnance. Weapons were mounted on seven hard points, four beneath the wings and three under the fuselage. ■

Painted in the desert pink colour scheme of Operation Granby, this Panavia Tornado was photographed at RAF Brize Norton in the autumn of 1991.
(Mike Freer Collection GNU Free Documentation License via Wikimedia Commons)

DEVELOPED IN A joint venture between the UK, Italy, and Germany, the Panavia Tornado is a two-seat fighter aircraft that served in multiple roles during the Gulf War. The air forces of the three partner nations each deployed the Tornado to the Middle East during Operation Desert Shield, and subsequently the aircraft executed a number of tactical strike missions while also engaging enemy air assets.

About 180 Tornado aircraft were deployed, including those operated by the Royal Saudi Air Force. Seventy of these belonged to the Royal Air Force (RAF) with 48 in the GR1 strike and 18 in the F3 air defence configurations, along with a detachment of GR1A reconnaissance planes. RAF air operations were nicknamed Operation Granby, and sources indicate that the RAF flew at least 1,500 and as many as 2,500 combat sorties during the air campaign. Tornado missions were regularly focused on hazardous low altitude attacks against enemy airfields and mid-level bombing runs against air defence emplacements.

This Panavia Tornado, a veteran of the Gulf War carrying 39 mission symbols, now resides in the RAF Museum, Hendon, London.
(Creative Commons Alan Wilson via Wikimedia Commons)

A Panavia Tornado of the Royal Saudi Air Force takes off. *(US Government via Wikimedia Commons)*

An F-117 Nighthawk stealth fighter releases a GBU-27 laser-guided munition.
(US Air Force via Wikimedia Commons)

F-117 NIGHTHAWK STEALTH FIGHTER

AMID THE ARRAY of advanced technology displayed by Coalition forces during Operation Desert Storm, perhaps no other combat system achieved greater fame and focus of media attention than the F-117 Nighthawk stealth fighter.

Research into stealth technology had begun more than a decade earlier with a USAF call for a jet fighter plane that could attack and destroy targets without being detected by enemy radar or other surveillance equipment. The result was the first operational stealth aircraft in history, and the F-117 took to the air for the first time in 1981. Developed by the famed Lockheed Skunk Works, the F-117 incorporated radar absorbent materials and design features that minimised its infrared signature, and the Air Force regularly denied its existence.

Only in November 1988, five years after the Nighthawk entered service, was the operational status of the F-117 acknowledged. Its combat debut took place in late 1989 during Operation Just Cause in Panama.

An F-117 stealth fighters refuels in the air from a KC-135 Stratotanker
(US Air Force via Wikimedia Commons)

The F-117 Nighthawk stealth fighter represented the leading edge of aerial technology during the Gulf War.
(US Air Force via Wikimedia Commons)

Retired from active service in 2008, the F-117 was a subsonic aircraft powered by two General Electric F404-F1D2 turbofan engines that generated a top speed of 684mph or Mach .92. The aircraft was crewed by a single pilot and carried an array of armament, including GBU laser-guided munitions with penetrator and blast/fragmentation warheads designed to hit runways, command and control facilities, and other high value targets, launched from two weapons bays. It was also capable of carrying nuclear weapons. It was intended as an attack aircraft rather than a dogfighting air superiority fighter.

A total of 59 F-117A combat aircraft were completed, and the record of the Nighthawk during the Gulf War included 1,271 combat sorties with a published 80% mission success rate. No combat losses or battle damage was experienced with the stealth fighter. According to Lockheed, the aircraft completed only 2% of the Coalition combat missions but covered 40% of the strategic targets identified. The F-117s dropped 2,077 bombs during the Gulf War, approximately 33% of the guided munitions expended.

Lockheed has published the assertion noted in an Air Force white paper on the air war that states: "The F-117 was the only airplane that the planners dared risk over downtown Baghdad." While some sceptics dispute this assertion, stating that other aircraft were involved in attacks on the Iraqi capital city, there is probably some credibility in the statement as it relates to the early hours of Coalition air operations. ∎

A-10 THUNDERBOLT

ALSO AFFECTIONATELY KNOWN as the Warthog, due to its decidedly non-aesthetically pleasing appearance, the Fairchild Republic A-10 Thunderbolt, named in honour of a famed US fighter plane of World War Two, rendered outstanding service to Coalition forces as a slow-flying subsonic tactical attack aircraft.

Both troops on the ground and the pilots who flew the A-10 were impressed with its array of firepower and effectiveness as a tank killer, Scud missile hunter, and destroyer of Iraqi fixed and mobile weaponry, and defensive positions. The A-10 was introduced in the autumn of 1977 and made its combat debut during Operation Desert Storm. Armed with a variety of ordnance, including up to 16,000lb of bombs, the 30mm General Electric GAU-8/A autocannon that fires a depleted uranium armour piercing shell and the AGM-65 Maverick missile, among other weapons, the A-10 flew 8,100 combat sorties during Desert Storm with 148 aircraft deployed including a dozen OA-10 forward air controller variants.

During Desert Storm, four Warthogs were lost to surface-to-air missiles, while 11 others sustained damage from anti-aircraft fire. Two aircraft were damaged heavily in combat and written off after returning to base. The Warthog became famous for its survivability, and some images of the damaged planes bear witness to its toughness. The A-10 pilot and cockpit are protected by a 'bathtub' of titanium aircraft armour, and the Warthog is said to withstand direct hits from enemy rounds up to 23mm.

The Thunderbolt and its pilots were sometimes the butt of humour with the plane's relatively slow speed (maximum 437mph) delivered by a pair of General Electric TF-34-GE-100

An A-10 fires its 30mm autocannon during exercises. The weapon was highly effective against Iraqi armour. *(US Air Force via Wikimedia Commons)*

turbofan engines with 9,000lb of thrust each. Its unflattering profile, however, became a welcome sight across the battlefield and endeared the A-10 to those who flew it. Shortcomings aside, the A-10 was proven effective in theatre. During one memorable encounter with Iraqi forces, a pair of A-10s destroyed 23 enemy tanks utilising the 30mm nose cannon and numerous anti-tank missiles. The Thunderbolt was also credited with shooting down two Iraqi helicopters with its 30mm cannon, the first incident occurring on February 8, 1991, when pilot Captain Robert Swain scored the victory over Kuwait.

The A-10 was also employed in protection and security operations to rescue downed airmen. During the course of the war, the plane reached a highly respectable 95.7% mission-capable rating. Despite persistent rumours that it is to be replaced, the Warthog

The tail section of this A-10 Thunderbolt of the 23rd Tactical Fighter Wing sustained combat damage from the detonation of an Iraqi surface-to-air missile.
(US Air Force via Wikimedia Commons)

remains in service and is the only aircraft deployed by the USAF that was specifically designed for the close air support role. ◼

This Fairchild Republic A-10 Thunderbolt is shown flying over the Middle Eastern desert. *(US Air Force via Wikimedia Commons)*

AH-64 APACHE

DEVELOPED IN THE mid-1970s in response to a US Army request for an anti-armour helicopter that would remain under its control, while fixed-wing close air support was the province of the US Air Force, the AH-64 Apache represented a great leap forwards in close air support technology. Hughes Aircraft and its successor McDonnell Douglas produced the AH-64 Apache from 1975, and the series has seen numerous upgrades, remaining in service today as more than 2,700 examples have been manufactured.

The AH-64 flew its first combat missions during 1989 Operation Just Cause in Panama, and 45% of the army's inventory, 274 helicopters, were deployed to the Middle East during Desert Storm. The Apache combat record was impressive as it has been credited with the destruction of more than 500 Iraqi armoured vehicles, including 278 tanks. In one memorable mission the mere presence of a pair of AH-64s overhead was enough to induce 400 Iraqi soldiers to surrender prior to the inception of the ground war.

Nevertheless, as it had been plagued with mechanical difficulties in peacetime, the Apache was not immune to continuing issues in the harsh desert climate. Maintenance and upkeep compelled the army to ground all Apaches not committed to the Middle East to supply spare parts, and heat and sand contributed to engine problems and other concerns. As a result, some sources relate that the AH-64 flew only 20% of the anticipated combat hours assigned. Others, however, assert that the Apache flew more than 18,000 combat hours with a 90% efficiency rating.

Still, the Apache was effective in its anti-armour role utilising a variety of armaments such as the 30mm M230 chain gun with 1,200 rounds of ammunition, Hellfire, Stinger, and Maverick missiles, and an array of rocket options – each system affixed to one of four hard points. These weapons were accurate due to the employment of state-of-the-art target acquisition apparatus highlighted by the Integrated Helmet and Display Sighting System (IHADSS) that allowed either of the two-man crew, pilot or gunner, to direct the 30mm M230 autocannon with head movements. The helicopter could operate in daylight or darkness, and in adverse weather conditions. The Apache was powered by a pair of General Electric T700-GE-701 turboshaft engines delivering a top speed of 182mph hour.

The AH-64 Apache was adept at dispatching Iraqi tanks and armoured vehicles, even before the ground war in Desert Storm. *(US Air Force via Wikimedia Commons)*

Hellfire missiles and Hydra rockets are affixed to hard points aboard the AH-64 Apache attack helicopter. *(Creative Commons David Monniaux via Wikimedia Commons)*

One major incident of friendly fire occurred on February 17, 1991, when an Apache destroyed a Bradley Fighting Vehicle and an M113 armoured personnel carrier, killing two American soldiers and wounding six.

With the beginning of the ground war, the AH-64 ranged approximately 20 miles inside Iraqi territory to destroy enemy strongpoints and concentrations of tanks and armoured vehicles. During Desert Storm, a single Apache was shot down by an Iraqi rocket-propelled grenade, but the crew survived and were rescued. Seven others sustained damage in combat. ■

An AH-64 Apache attack helicopter is shown amid its array of advanced weaponry. *(US Army via Wikimedia Commons)*

A submarine-launched Tomahawk cruise missile breaks the surface and streaks skywards. *(National Museum of the US Navy via Wikimedia Commons)*

TOMAHAWK
CRUISE MISSILE

THE CULMINATION OF a research and development effort that had gained significant momentum during the 1970s, the Tomahawk cruise missile made its combat debut during Operation Desert Storm. Travelling at a cruising speed of 550mph and carrying a 1,000lb warhead, the Tomahawk was designed to hit high value targets such as Iraqi command and control centres, concentrations of arms and supplies, and even Saddam Hussein's presidential palace.

The cruise missile, therefore, engaged these targets with precision without the risk of human life being required to go in harm's way to accomplish such hazardous missions. In addition to executing such strikes, the Tomahawk was involved in the first co-ordinated missions between manned attack aircraft and smart weapons in military history.

Developed and manufactured by General Dynamics and its successors, the BGM-109 Tomahawk Land Attack Missile (TLAM) was one of several variants available from launch platforms such as surface ships and submarines of the US Navy, as well as B-52 bomber air launched and ground-launched systems. Approximately 21ft long and weighing 1½ tons, the cruise missile of Gulf War fame was launched vertically from tubes aboard warships or horizontally from submarines, a booster rocket gaining altitude giving way to a turbofan engine.

The accuracy of the Tomahawk was derived from three separate guidance systems. The inertial guidance system stabilised the missile and set its course. Once the Tomahawk reached land, the TERCOM (Terrain Contour Matching) system took over and continually matched altitude and course readings stored aboard to images of land features observed. From there, the Digital Scene Matching Area Correlator (DSMAC) system compared stored photos of the target to images being observed to direct the missile accurately while flying at low altitude, 100 to 300ft.

Press reports at the time of the Gulf War touted the Tomahawk's accuracy with statements that

A Tomahawk cruise missile streaks from its launch tube aboard the battleship USS *Missouri* towards a target in Iraq, January 17, 1991. *(US Navy via Wikimedia Commons)*

a missile could be fired in New York harbour and pass through the goalpost at Robert F Kennedy stadium (home of the Washington professional football team). Through the course of the Gulf War, nearly 300 Tomahawks were fired, and initial reports asserted accuracy as high as 90%. However, subsequent studies have cast some doubt on those results, reducing the purported performance to 50 to 60%.

According to available data, 288 to 297 missiles were fired, a dozen of these from submarines and the remainder from surface ships including cruisers and destroyers, and the battleships *Wisconsin* and *Missouri*. Of these, it is believed that nine failed to exit their launch tubes, six malfunctioned and fell into the sea, and between two and six were shot down by air defences. Nevertheless, the Tomahawk became a symbol of advancing technology during Desert Storm, and in addition to its combat capability, its psychological impact was substantial. ■

The guided missile cruiser USS *Normandy* fires a Tomahawk cruise missile against a target in Iraq. *(US Navy via Wikimedia Commons)*

MLRS

MLRS rockets streak across the desert towards their targets during the Gulf War.
(Creative Commons Don Brunett via Wikimedia Commons)

A US Army MLRS fires during exercises in 1982. *(US Army via Wikimedia Commons)*

DEVELOPED IN THE late 1970s in response to a US Army Missile Command request for proposals for a new general support rocket system, the MLRS (Multiple Launch Rocket System) made its combat debut during the Gulf War. Its deployment was successful to the extent that Iraqi prisoners revealed their nickname for the system – steel rain.

Utilising the chassis of the Bradley Fighting Vehicle, the MLRS launcher carried a pair of six-round pods containing M77 rockets with payloads of anti-tank mines or 644 bomblets that can be distributed across a target area of more than four acres. If fired simultaneously, a complete salvo of 12 rockets would theoretically cover an area of 30 acres. The system is also capable of firing the Army Tactical Missile System (ATACMS) against certain stationary, fixed targets. Since its initial delivery to the US Army in 1983, the MLRS has undergone numerous upgrades, and has been utilised by numerous countries, including Great Britain and other NATO allies, Ukraine, Japan, and Saudi Arabia, among others.

During the Gulf War, the United States deployed more than 230 examples of the MLRS, and Britain an additional 16. In support of the XVIII Airborne Corps, the 6th Battalion, 27th Field Artillery was the first to fire the MLRS during Operation Desert Storm. Iraqi surface-to-air missile (SAM) sites were suppressed using the ATACMS during the opening hours of the Coalition air campaign to degrade enemy air defences, and in a single engagement three MLRS batteries engaged 24 separate targets while firing 287 rockets in five minutes. The batteries expended a quantity of ordnance during that short period that would have required standard field artillery batteries more than an hour to replicate. The MLRS proved effective in preparatory bombardment of Iraqi fixed defences, artillery and missile sites, and personnel and armour concentrations.

When the ground war commenced in February 1991, the 4th Battalion, 27th Field Artillery Regiment fired 312 rockets in predawn darkness during the largest single support effort of the conflict and the largest nocturnal mission of its kind in history. By the end of Operation Desert Storm, estimates of at least 6,000 to more than 9,600 MLRS rockets and 32 ATACMS missiles had been fired. MLRS batteries accounted for roughly 11 to 17% of all artillery rounds fired in the Gulf War. ∎

This MLRS battery is shown moving into firing position during exercises.
(US Government via Wikimedia Commons)

SCUD MISSILE

Rescue workers search through the ruins of a building in Israel after the impact of a Scud missile. *(Creative Commons National Photo Collection of Israel via Wikimedia Commons)*

THE SOVIET-MADE Scud series of tactical ballistic missiles posed a significant threat, not only to Coalition forces during the Gulf War, but also to civilians in Saudi Arabia, Israel, and Kuwait.

Dating back to the early days of the Cold War, the Scud was a largely inaccurate weapon that was nevertheless capable of wreaking significant damage to targets with its high explosive, fragmentation, chemical or nuclear warhead. Most significantly, it served as a powerful terror weapon. Political implications followed it when Saddam Hussein authorised firing Scuds against Israel, hoping to spark retaliation that would fracture the tenuous co-operation of Arab countries with the US-led alliance arrayed against him.

By the time of the Gulf War, the Iraqis had deployed the Scud-B, along with the modified Al Hussein, Al Hijarah, and Al Abbas variants with longer range and first fired during the 1980-88 war with Iran. At the beginning of the Gulf War, Iraq was known to possess at least 200 mobile launchers, and 88 Scuds were fired against Coalition targets during the course of the fighting, 42 into Saudi Arabia and 46 into Israeli air space. Elimination of the Scud threat was identified as a priority, and more than 2,500 air sorties were conducted against both fixed and mobile launch sites. Units of the British Special Air Service and the US Special Forces, sometimes inserted by helicopter, hunted the Scud launchers on the ground.

During the war, numerous Scud missiles were destroyed in the air by the US-designed Patriot missile air defence system. However, the Scuds were large and debris regularly fell into populated areas and caused significant damage. At least 230 people were injured in Scud attacks, and the greatest loss was suffered when a single missile eluded air defences on February 25, 1991, and struck an American barracks in Dhahran Saudi Arabia, killing 28 US military personnel and wounding 100, primarily members of the army's 14th Quartermaster Detachment.

Compounding the Coalition challenge to suppress and eliminate the Scud threat, the Iraqis used shoot and scoot tactics with their mobile launchers aboard Soviet-built MAZ-543 vehicles and other transport. The Scud was just over 34ft-long and carried warheads ranging from 650lb with the Al Abbas to 1,000lb with the Al Hussein. Its range of up to 400 miles brought significant areas of Coalition operations within reach. By the end of the Gulf War, an estimated 19 Scud launchers were still operational in the Iraqi arsenal. ■

This Scud B missile launch system resides today in a museum in Russia. *(Creative Commons One half 3544 via Wikimedia Commons)*

Soldiers inspect the remnants of an Iraqi Scud missile fired during the Gulf War. *(US Department of Defense via Wikimedia Commons)*

REPORTING THE WAR

The Al Rashid Hotel is a prominent structure in the heart of Baghdad.
(Creative Commons James Gordon via Wikimedia Commons)

"**S**OMETHING IS HAPPENING outside... the skies over Baghdad have been illuminated." The perspective was remarkable. When CNN (Cable News Network) correspondent Bernard Shaw made his first live report on the outbreak of the Gulf War, he did so from inside the Al Rashid Hotel in downtown Baghdad.

"If there had been one indiscriminately dropped bomb or one misdirected bomb, if the hotel had been hit, that would have been it," Shaw later declared. His statement was accurate. Along with CNN reporters Peter Arnett and John Holliman, Shaw made television news – and indeed journalism – history. Live reports from the Iraqi capital reached homes in the United States and around the world, allowing viewers to witness the prosecution of the air assault and later events of the conflict in real time.

In presenting their historic reports, Shaw, Arnett, and Holliman made CNN a dominating force in news coverage, eclipsing at times the tremendous influence of the big three networks,

Arthur Kent discusses the location of a camera during a report from the Burgan oil field in 1991.
(Creative Commons Mblegacy via Wikimedia Commons)

Shown with CBS News anchor Dan Rather (left), CNN newsman Peter Arnett was in Baghdad at the outbreak of Desert Storm. *(US Government via Wikimedia Commons)*

Television journalist Arthur Kent became an international celebrity reporting on the Gulf War. *(Creative Commons Arthur Kent via Wikimedia Commons)*

on the street, and eventually the very negative comments of the minders (Iraqi government handlers) themselves. They were increasingly unhappy. I mean the whole CNN crew was being pulled aside in hallways and given, you know, complaints about what was going on in the government. We had to be very careful about how we handled all this information."

US television network coverage was anchored by familiar faces: Peter Jennings of ABC, Tom Brokaw of NBC, and Dan Rather of CBS. During one memorable exchange, ABC reporter Gary Shepherd was describing the quiet scene in Baghdad but seconds later, the calm was shattered with flashes and explosions on the horizon as Coalition air assets attacked. NBC correspondent Mike Boettcher was at Dhahran Air Base in Saudi Arabia when he noticed a heightened level of activity. A few minutes later, Brokaw received reports of strikes inside Iraq that signalled the beginning of the Desert Storm air campaign.

Media correspondents from around the world filed reports from the Middle East. In Britain the BBC established Radio 4 News FM with an

Bernard Shaw of CNN delivered groundbreaking live reports from Baghdad. *(US Department of Defense via Wikimedia Commons)*

eventually led to the outbreak of armed conflict. Arnett was particularly the subject of scrutiny after his reporting included an interview with embattled Iraqi leader Saddam Hussein. He further covered the Coalition bombing of a facility that was believed to be a poison gas factory, despite Iraqi claims that it was a baby food manufacturing plant. He also reported on the bombing of a purported civilian air raid shelter, which Coalition intelligence had identified as a military command and control centre, producing non-combatant casualties.

"What did these reports finally add up to?" Arnett later assessed. "This is of course in addition to our visual reports or video of the obvious stories, the civilian casualties, the atmosphere of Baghdad in the streets, the many quotes we got from people along the way. I think what these reports finally added up to, we were able to chart the increasing – well, the rapid deterioration of Iraqi society and the frustration of the average man

ABC, CBS, and NBC, that had previously dominated televised news reporting in the United States. Utilising a uniquely installed communication line with satellite access, the group made reliable transmissions, while other networks sometimes had difficulty maintaining contact via conventional telephone lines.

When their first reports came through on January 16, 1991, the bombs were literally falling on the city of Baghdad. Shaw sought shelter under a desk and noted that an American cruise missile had literally flown past his window on the hotel's ninth floor. He shuttled to and from a bomb shelter at the Al Rashid and stated matter-of-factly during a lull in the bombardment: "You wouldn't know there's life outside these windows…We can see there are fires off in the distance… It's eerily silent."

The CNN trio was also the source of controversy after being granted permission to remain in Baghdad during the heightening tension that

When Desert Storm erupted, reporters and civilians scurried for cover within the Al Rashid Hotel in Baghdad. *(Creative Commons James Gordon via Wikimedia Commons)*

18-hour rolling news reporting format, which led to the initiation of BBC Radio 5 Live. ITN and BBC television reporters ventured to the front lines to report on the war, transmitting live feeds and breaking news. Newspapers carried extensive reports and blared headlines on a daily basis. More than 700 media representatives registered for credentials with the US Military Joint Information Bureau in Dhahran.

During the entire Desert Shield/Storm crisis, media access was rather tightly controlled on an official basis. In sharp contrast to the relative freedom of movement reporters had experienced during the Vietnam War a quarter century earlier, media representatives were largely restricted to pool coverage, an agreed upon process by which the military and the media were supposedly poised to maintain and enhance the security surrounding ongoing operations, possibly improve the quality and immediacy of news coverage, and minimise the risk of injury among the press corps. In practice, the pool system was quite restrictive. Media representatives were constantly escorted by military personnel who reportedly told them where they could and could not go, while limiting access to certain individuals for interviews, and even supplying or approving questions that might be asked.

Despite the restrictions placed on individual reporters, some were determined to seek the front lines and found themselves in the midst of the conflict. Popularly known as "pool busters", these reporters included Elizabeth Colton, a special correspondent for Mutual Broadcasting and NBC Radio News. Colton was reporting near the Kuwaiti frontier on February 26, 1991, when a group of 11 Iraqi soldiers emerged from hiding, offered their weapons to her, and surrendered. Colton was unarmed. Taken aback, she led the group of captives to a nearby holding area for prisoners. Ranging forward of the Coalition ground forces, ABC News reporter Forrest Sawyer glimpsed some of the first Iraqi soldiers to surrender during the lightning ground advance of Desert Storm, and took photos of their rapid capitulation. CBS News reporter Bob Simon and

BBC reporter John Simpson answers questions about his journalism career. *(Creative Commons Sobranie-Cocktail via Wikimedia Commons)*

his entire crew were captured by Iraqi forces and remained in captivity for six weeks until their release was secured by Soviet envoys.

BBC correspondents John Simpson and Bob Simpson ignored orders leave Baghdad. One of their subsequent reports captured a cruise missile hurtling down a street in the Iraqi capital and, upon reaching an intersection, making a left turn towards its pre-programmed target.

The Gulf War spawned a bevy of celebrities, who became household names in the US and UK during the course of the conflict. One of the most famous reporters was Arthur Kent of NBC News. Kent was a good looking 37-year-old Canadian-born journalist who appeared live from Dhahran wearing a distinctive leather jacket, the desert wind blowing through his dark hair. Air raid sirens and the tracks of missiles, explosions overhead and at a distance,

punctuated Kent's reports and earned him the sexually charged nickname the 'Scud Stud'.

On January 20, 1991, as Iraqi Scud missiles were launched and US-made Patriot anti-missile missiles were unleashed against them, Kent reported: "Hello, New York! They're firing Patriots! this is not a drill!"

ABC News anchor Peter Jennings was a familiar face during unprecedented coverage of the Gulf War. *(Creative Commons Peabody Awards via Wikimedia Commons)*

NBC journalist Brad Willis, a veteran of Gulf War coverage, posed for this photo in the mid-1980s in Afghanistan. *(Creative Commons Brad Willis Archive via Wikimedia Commons)*

Kent recalled his energetic narrative in an attempt to gain air time. "Suddenly we had a story falling on our heads, and we had the ability to report it in real time. I was trying to get their attention because I knew in the control room they were watching about 40 monitors around the world, including the football game. I felt good that we did not make mistakes and we did not compromise security for anyone in that area when we reported the Patriots intercepting some of the incoming Scuds. You could see some of the debris explode in the dark and send up a glow. We were about 200 miles from anything even remotely approaching the front. We were reporting under the strictest controls US journalists had ever faced. The pool system that hampered us in the first Gulf War should not be forced on journalists again, other than in exceptional circumstances."

Reporting the Gulf War revealed military operations in real time while also demonstrating some of the most advanced weapons technology in the world, and the military held daily briefings on the progress of the Desert Storm offensive. General Norman Schwarzkopf, commander of Coalition forces, held daily media briefings and proved adept at his handling of the press. The briefings were often highlighted with video footage of smart weapons using guidance systems to home in and strike. Targets would be observed on the video until the moment of impact when the screen went blank.

Schwarzkopf's witty banter captivated audiences during the briefings, and he once quipped: "As far as Saddam Hussein

NBC News anchor Tom Brokaw interviews General Norman Schwarzkopf during the Gulf War. *(US Department of Defense via Wikimedia Commons)*

being a great military strategist, he is neither a strategist, nor is he schooled in the operational arts, nor is he a tactician, nor is he a general, nor is he a soldier. Other than that, he's a great military man." Such commentary was sublime fodder for news outlets in print, radio, and television.

One of the defining moments of the Gulf War occurred during a memorable Schwarzkopf briefing. Again, the highly quotable officer was in his element, asking reporters to view a video clip. "I'm now going to show you a picture of the luckiest man in Iraq," the general smiled. "Keep your eye on the crosshairs," he advised as a bridge located somewhere in Iraq came into focus on the monitor. A truck rolled into view, and the driver began to cross the bridge even as the pilot of a Coalition combat aircraft initiated an attack on the span. The truck sped across the bridge and passed straight through the pilot's aiming apparatus.

"And now, in his rear-view mirror," the General grinned. The pilot's ordnance release was right on time and target. Just as the truck cleared the bridge, a massive explosion marked the destruction of the span in smoke, flame and debris. The driver had crossed safely – barely escaping with his life.

Such was just one example of Schwarzkopf's deft handling of the media, gathered and hungry for sights and sound bites, the awe inspiring accuracy of modern weapons technology, and the survival of a single individual, lucky to still be alive.

Reporting the Gulf War opened new frontiers, enlightening the public and posing questions for the future of journalism in wartime. ◼

US Defense Secretary Dick Cheney addresses the media during a Gulf War press conference. *(US Navy via Wikimedia Commons)*

Italian journalist Sandro Petrone reported from Kuwait City in the aftermath of Desert Storm. *(Public Domain Sandro Petrone via Wikimedia Commons)*

WAR AT SEA

The battleship USS *Wisconsin* fires a Tomahawk cruise missile in daylight Desert Storm operations. *(US Navy via Wikimedia Commons)*

IT WAS NO contest. And the Coalition naval forces that dispatched the bulk of the Iraqi navy in about four days did so with precision and purpose.

Months before the outbreak of Gulf War hostilities, naval assets had been the first military instrument of consequence in the Middle East. While the US Navy had maintained a constant presence in the region, it was joined eventually by warships and support vessels from 18 other countries to enforce the economic sanctions imposed on Iraq by the United Nations through blockade efforts that denied Saddam Hussein the essentials to sustain his war machine.

With the build-up of Desert Shield and the beginning of the Desert Storm air war, US Navy planes flew more than 33,000 sorties, many of them covering great distances from the Red Sea and the Arabian Sea, with durations of five hours or more. But the combat air patrol, reconnaissance and surveillance, and strike missions flown by navy pilots, were only one aspect of a multi-faceted role played by the Coalition naval forces.

Within hours of the Iraqi invasion of Kuwait, the aircraft carrier USS *Independence* and her battle group were ordered to the Arabian Sea to bolster assets already in the region.

The carrier USS *Eisenhower* transited the Suez Canal from the Mediterranean and took up position in the Red Sea, while the carrier USS *Saratoga*, battleship USS *Wisconsin*, and the helicopter assault carrier USS *Inchon* with a battalion of combat ready Marines aboard, weighed anchor for the Middle East.

Aircraft carriers have long been acknowledged as primary projectors of military might and air power anywhere in the world, and by the time Desert Storm began, six carriers of the US Navy and complementary battle groups had reached the area of operations, including USS *Theodore Roosevelt*, USS *America*, USS *John F Kennedy*, and USS *Saratoga* in the Red Sea with USS *Midway* and USS *Ranger* adding power in the Persian Gulf. US naval strength in the Kuwaiti theatre peaked at 120 ships, more than 80 of them warships and 15 of these nuclear powered. Altogether, more than 200 Coalition warships participated in the Gulf War, with at least 15 cruisers and nearly 70 destroyers, frigates and smaller craft involved. The Royal Navy contributed a 33-ship task force to the Gulf War, its largest deployment since the Falklands War of 1982.

Worthy of note among these were the two World War Two vintage battleships USS *Wisconsin* and USS *Missouri*. These venerable vessels, both commissioned in 1944, had been the subject of controversy, retired from service and then re-commissioned in the 1980s. They were modernised to fire the state-of-the-art Tomahawk cruise missile and were provided with other new weaponry, but maintained their 16in main batteries, which they had not fired in anger since the Korean War.

During Desert Storm, the round-the-clock bombardment of Iraqi military targets was

The Royal Navy Type 42 destroyer HMS *Gloucester* was heavily involved in Desert Storm operations. *(Creative Commons Tony Hisgett via Wikimedia Commons)*

The destroyer USS *Paul F Foster* fired the first Tomahawk cruise missile in combat. *(US Navy via Wikimedia Commons)*

The helicopter assault carrier USS *Tripoli* sits in drydock in Dubai undergoing repairs after striking a mine in the Persian Gulf. *(US Navy via Wikimedia Commons)*

In this photo taken from the cruiser USS *Princeton*, an Iraqi mine floats menacingly in the Persian Gulf. *(US Navy via Wikimedia Commons)*

accomplished from the sea as at least a half-dozen Aegis-class cruisers, armed with 200 Tomahawks and the latest air defence systems, ranged across the Red Sea. Escort vessels plied the waters of the Persian Gulf to neutralise Iraqi anti-aircraft fire from converted oil platforms, and destroyed enemy minelaying and patrol craft that threatened the security of Coalition forces with their supply of French-made Exocet anti-ship missiles.

The US Navy made history during the Gulf War as the destroyer USS *Paul F Foster* launched the first Tomahawk missile in combat on January 17, 1991, from its station in the Persian Gulf.

Two days later, the Tomahawk and the US Navy made headlines with the first submarine-launched cruise missile, fired from the Los Angeles-class attack submarine USS *Louisville* in the Red Sea. The launch was revealed to the world during a subsequent briefing in Riyadh, Saudi Arabia. Although submarine actions were hardly ever discussed openly, Air Force Lieutenant Colonel Mike Scott, the briefing officer, made an exception "...to document a significant event in naval history." A Pentagon official added: "A lack of fanfare is the measure of submariners' success. The only time you would know that it's there is when the Tomahawk breaks the water." A total of eight attack submarines were believed to be operating in surrounding waters during Desert Storm, but their overall presence was never confirmed.

The complexity of daily naval operations required substantial co-ordination, and aboard the command-and-control ship USS *Blue Ridge*, Admiral Stanley Arthur led those responsible for choreographing bombing sorties against strategic targets, tactical support for ground forces, preparations for a potential amphibious assault by Marines against the Kuwaiti coastline, defending against the Iraqi navy, and keeping operational waters free of enemy mines. At the same time, US Coast Guard personnel were on alert to seize any Iraqi naval vessels that might be captured intact, while SEALS (the Navy's Sea, Air, and Land special forces) were available for covert missions as well as direct combat with enemy forces. The Marines trained continually for amphibious landings, while rapid deployment and landward sustainment capabilities were refined in theatre.

Although the Iraqi navy was estimated to include only four guided-missile frigates, six corvettes, 21 patrol boats, eight minesweepers, and other smaller craft, it nevertheless posed a threat to the Coalition forces at sea. While pre-emptive air strikes were aimed at neutralising the Exocet and Chinese-made Silkworm missile launch sites that might target Coalition assets, the Royal Navy destroyer HMS *Gloucester* demonstrated its defensive capabilities while riding 'shotgun' for USS *Missouri* as the battleship fired its 16in guns against shore targets. A pair of Silkworms were detected speeding toward the Coalition warships. One of these crashed into the

The Saudi guided-missile patrol boat *Faisal* sank an Iraqi vessel with a Harpoon missile. *(US Navy via Wikimedia Commons)*

Damage from an Iraqi influence mine is visible in the wrinkled hull of the cruiser USS *Princeton*. (US Navy via Wikimedia Commons)

sea. *Gloucester* engaged the other with a Sea Dart anti-missile missile and blasted it from the sky.

Royal Navy spokesman Commander John Tighe quipped: "Undoubtedly there are some relieved sailors aboard another Coalition vessel due to the quick action of a radar operator aboard HMS *Gloucester*."

Naval personnel were tasked with clearing those oil platforms which the Iraqis had turned into fortified positions that harassed Coalition aircraft with small arms and anti-aircraft fire. On January 18, the frigate USS *Nicholas* and a Kuwaiti patrol boat were joined by a pair of US Army helicopters to wrest control of nine of these platforms. Nicholas blew apart one Iraqi patrol boat and engaged the enemy soldiers on the platforms for three hours. A dozen Iraqi soldiers eventually surrendered to the Marine detachment aboard *Nicholas*, and these were believed to be the first enemy combatants taken prisoner in the conflict.

Six days later, the US Navy liberated the first piece of Kuwaiti territory, the tiny island of Qaruh. The frigate USS *Curts* crew observed the island, only 400yds wide, which had been identified as an enemy intelligence gathering post. Suddenly, an alarm was raised.

"The first gut-wrenching experience came about 20 minutes after we went to general quarters," recalled Commander Glenn Montgomery at a subsequent briefing. "We got the first report of aircraft inbound... three Iraqi aircraft over the land mass headed in our direction." Fifteen tense minutes ticked by, and the contact faded. "I don't know what the enemy did," concluded Montgomery, "but honest to goodness at that point I really didn't care as long as he didn't keep coming in at me."

Curts dispatched a boarding party that secured an Iraqi minelayer that had been strafed by A-6 Intruder attack planes from the Theodore Roosevelt while Marines and

A Royal Navy Westland Lynx helicopter flies over the Greek destroyer HS *Kriezis*. (US Department of Defense via Wikimedia Commons)

Navy SEALS quickly took possession of Qaruh. Fifty-one Iraqis were captured.

On the night of January 24, the Saudi guided-missile patrol boat Faisal detected a blip on its radar and sent a helicopter aloft to investigate. After the vessel was identified as an Iraqi minelayer operating in Saudi territorial waters, Faisal launched a single Harpoon

The hospital ship USNS *Comfort* was deployed to the Persian Gulf during Desert Shield/Storm. (US Department of Defense via Wikimedia Commons)

The French aircraft carrier *Clemenceau* lies moored in port during Desert Shield. *(US Department of Defense via Wikimedia Commons)*

The Dutch frigate *Jacob van Heemskerck* draws alongside the aircraft carrier USS *Ranger* during Desert Storm. *(US Department of Defense via Wikimedia Commons)*

crowded and encounters did occur. On February 18, within ten miles and two-and-a-half hours of one another, the helicopter assault carrier USS *Tripoli* and the Aegis missile cruiser USS *Princeton* were damaged by mines. Tripoli was serving as the flagship of the Coalition mine hunting effort, but at 4.35am, a floating contact mine tore a 20ft by 20ft gash in the ship's hull.

Tripoli quickly settled 3ft lower in the water. Damage control parties secured the ship, and rescuers brought personnel overcome by acrid fumes to safety. Miraculously, although the ship was carrying 1,300 combat Marines, only four men were slightly injured.

The 9,460-ton *Princeton* was damaged by an influence mine, which exploded by the ship's stern, damaged its rudder, and sprung leaks around the port propeller shaft. The powerful explosion lifted the ship partially out of the water. Yet there was no hole, the only external evidence being a wrinkle in the hull.

After a few hours, *Tripoli* was pronounced "fully mission capable" and resumed station prior to later withdrawal. Three crewmen were wounded, one of them in serious condition. They were all transferred to a nearby Royal Navy vessel for treatment. *Princeton* was ordered to port for repairs.

Throughout the seven months of Desert Shield/Storm, mines were a continual threat. Close encounters became the order of the day, and 160 contact mines were detected. HMS *Gloucester* passed within 15ft of what appeared to be a floating explosive in one near miss. Captain James Buckner of the destroyer USS *Turner* remembered sighting a suspicious object on the surface. "In the binoculars it looked like a mine," he smiled. "It turned out to be a tied-up bin bag. You just can't take any chances."

One of the most significant aspects of the Coalition naval presence was the establishment of shipborne medical facilities. The hospital ships USNS *Mercy* and USNS *Comfort* were on station in the Persian Gulf with 2,000 patient beds and 24 operating suites ready for treatment of a flood of combat casualties that never came. ◼

missile at a distance of 22nm. Its impact left the minelayer a blazing hulk. The Iraqi navy was systematically pummelled by Coalition naval forces. Co-ordinated attacks from air and sea were executed with telling effect.

The decisive naval encounter of the Gulf War is remembered as the Battle of Bubiyan, January 29 to February 2. Remnants of the battered Iraqi navy were caught attempting to flee to Iran between Bubiyan Island and the Shatt al-Arab waterway, and Westland Lynx helicopters of the Royal Navy played a primary role in the destruction that ensued. A reported 21 Iraqi vessels were sunk and two others damaged, including patrol and landing ships, fast attack craft, minelayers, and minesweepers. The Lynx crews skilfully deployed their Sea Skua missiles in multiple attacks, while a Canadian F/A-18 Hornet aircraft was thought to have despatched another enemy craft. The highest intensity of the fighting occurred during running engagements over a 13-hour period.

Despite all efforts to clear operational areas of mines, inevitably the sea became

The Canadian operational support ship HMCS *Protecteur* plies the waters of the Persian Gulf. *(US Navy via Wikimedia Commons)*

F-16 Fighting Falcon and F-15 Eagle fighters of the 4th Fighter Wing, USAF, fly above flaming oil facilities in the Kuwaiti desert. *(US Air Force via Wikimedia Commons)*

AERIAL ONSLAUGHT

This Soviet-built Sukhoi Su-25 attack plane was destroyed on the ground by Coalition air power. *(US Army via Wikimedia Commons)*

PRESIDENT GEORGE HW Bush announced to the world: "The liberation of Kuwait has begun." Approximately two hours earlier, in the pre-dawn darkness of January 17, 1991, Coalition air forces initiated a massive campaign to degrade the comprehensive capability of the Iraqi military to wage war.

Unprecedented in size and scope, fury and precision, the five-week aerial onslaught succeeded in blinding the Iraqi command-and-control capabilities. It took out vital radar and anti-aircraft emplacements, destroyed Iraqi tanks and armoured vehicles in the field, torched the Iraqi air force and compelled some pilots to flee to neighbouring Iran, and thoroughly demoralised many of the Iraqi soldiers arrayed against Coalition forces on the ground.

During Operations Desert Shield and Desert Storm, the Coalition amassed more than 3,000 fixed-wing and rotary aircraft of many types to carry out the varied missions laid before the commanders. More than 60% of these were combat aircraft, and more than 2,400 were American, the remainder contributed by the British Royal Air Force and those of France, Italy, Saudi Arabia and other partners.

The architect of the air campaign was US General Charles Horner, a veteran combat pilot of the Vietnam War. Horner defined the mission of the air assets succinctly – to swiftly gain air superiority, degrade the combat efficiency of the enemy forces in the field, deprive them of their eyes and ears through precision strikes against command-and-control centres, and to inflict substantial casualties on the opposing forces to minimise resistance to the upcoming ground phase of Operation Desert Storm.

Although sources vary as to the first hostile shots fired during the air war, many historians attribute these to the AH-64 Apache attack helicopters of the US Army special operations Task Force Normandy, which took out early warning radar sites deep inside western Iraq beginning just before 3am local time, paving the way for McDonnell Douglas F-15 Eagle strike fighters to sweep through the gaping window and attack a variety of targets inside enemy territory.

On the first day of the air onslaught, Coalition planes flew 1,000 combat sorties and dropped at least 2,200 tons of ordnance, conventional and smart weapons. The pace increased substantially during the following days, with missions reaching a staggering 2,000 to 3,000 every 24 hours. When the Coalition strikes began, the results were immediately visible.

The deployment of the Tomahawk cruise missile was historic, and these precision-guided weapons were seen by reporters in downtown Baghdad. CNN correspondent John Holliman reported: "The sky is just brightly lighted with all these tracer rounds. Some are red. Some are white. We can see explosions from these weapons... Now there's a huge fire we've just seen that is due west of our position. And we just heard... Whoa! Holy cow! That was a large air burst that we saw. It was filling the sky."

Numerous Tomahawks were fired from US Navy surface vessels, as well as the eight attack submarines operating offshore. Others were delivered from the air in one of the most secretive endeavours of the burgeoning offensive.

The Boeing B-52 Stratofortress was an icon of the Cold War. Already in service for decades, the platform performed magnificently during Desert Storm and completed a tremendous test of endurance both for plane and aircrew. Flying from Barksdale Air Force Base, Louisiana, seven B-52s of the USAF's 596th Bomb Squadron had trained for six months to execute Operation Senior Surprise, the delivery of the AGM-86 CALCM (Conventional Air Launched Cruise Missile), the first such weapon to utilise GPS

The Grumman A-6 Intruder attack aircraft flew from US Navy aircraft carriers and Marine bases on land during the Gulf War. *(US Air Force via Wikimedia Commons)*

The General Dynamics EF-111 Raven electronic warfare plane suppressed Iraqi radar and anti-aircraft defences during Coalition flight operations. *(US Government via Wikimedia Commons)*

The Fairchild Republic A-10 Thunderbolt, nicknamed Warthog, was a formidable ground attack aircraft throughout the Gulf War. *(US Air Force via Wikimedia Commons)*

(Global Positioning System) technology to fix and strike targets with a 1,000lb warhead.

"I was first informed of the mission in August 1990, and then we had six months to train on the new weapon," related Warren Ward, a co-pilot aboard a B-52 during the mission that the airmen dubbed 'Operation Secret Squirrel'. As the mission commenced, the B-52s flew over the Atlantic to refuel from KC-135 tankers flying from the Azores. After reaching the Mediterranean, they again refuelled from KC-10 tankers out of Moron Air Base, Spain. After reaching the Red Sea and the Arabian desert, the Stratofortresses approached Saudi air space and unleashed 35 cruise missiles in a staggered firing sequence. At least 28 were believed to have struck their targets, including the Al-Mussaib Thermal power plant in Babi province, south of Baghdad.

All seven B-52s returned safely to Barksdale, their mission having covered 14,000 miles in 35 hours, 24 minutes, a new world record for the longest bombing mission in history. But Secret Squirrel was

Two-seat F-15E Strike Eagle aircraft sit ready for upcoming missions at a desert air base. *(US Air Force via Wikimedia Commons)*

A squadron of RAF Panavia Tornado fighters on the tarmac at its home base. Tornado pilots executed hazardous attacks on Iraqi air bases in the Gulf War. *(Creative Commons Andy Marks-ManxAirPix via Wikimedia Commons)*

only one dimension of the awe-inspiring execution of the Gulf War air component.

Among the earliest penetrators of Iraqi air space were the state-of-the-art stealth Lockheed F-117 Nighthawk attack aircraft. Approximately 30 of these planes from the 37th Tactical Fighter Wing, virtually undetectable by operational radar, swooped towards their targets, including the Rasheed Street Communications Centre in downtown Baghdad. Precision munitions were loosed with incredible accuracy, destroying not only this primary command and control centre, but others in the Iraqi capital too. The F-117s were reported to have flown as many as 95% of the manned missions against Baghdad itself, where strong anti-aircraft defences were located.

Two versions of the F-15 Eagle, the F-15C air superiority fighter and the two-seat F-15E strike aircraft, were aloft during the air assault. The surrounding skies were swept for enemy fighter planes, such as the Soviet-built MiG-23, MiG-25, and MiG-29, and attack aircraft such as the French Dassault Mirage F-1 and Soviet Sukhoi Su-22, Su-24, and Su-25. Along with the F-15s, F-16 Fighting Falcons performed in the attack role, joined by US Navy A-6 and A-7 and F/A-18s flying from carriers in the Red Sea and Persian Gulf. The RAF Panavia Tornado was ideally suited for attacks against Iraqi air bases, and these intrepid pilots flew hazardous missions to render runways unusable with specialised ordnance, as well as blasting adjacent facilities and enemy aircraft on the ground.

Numerous additional aircraft types were involved in the air war in support and attack roles. Essential to its success were those forward of the attack formations responsible for jamming Iraqi radar and rendering surveillance, fire control, and fighter interdiction ineffective. Radar jamming US Navy EA-6B Prowlers used electronic countermeasures to pinpoint and stifle enemy radar sites and signals. The

Grumman F-14 Tomcat carrier-based US Navy fighters refuel from an airborne tanker. *(US Department of Defense via Wikimedia Commons)*

US Air Force General Charles Horner commanded the Coalition air effort in Desert Storm. *(US National Archives and Records Administration via Wikimedia Commons)*

Both British and French airmen flew the SEPECAT Jaguar attack aircraft during the Gulf War. *(US National Archives and Records Administration via Wikimedia Commons)*

venerable F4G Wild Weasel, surface-to-air missile attack variant of the Vietnam-era F-4 Phantom fighter, took out Iraqi missile sites and paved the way for aggressive strike missions. The EF-111 Raven, electronic countermeasure variant of the F-111 fighter bomber, released electronic 'noise' to disorient enemy radar operators, while early warning aircraft such as the Navy E-2C AWACS (airborne warning and control system) and the Air Force E-3 eyed enemy air installations for any indication of fighter take-offs and directed airborne 'traffic'.

During the first 48 hours of the air war, Coalition aircraft flew approximately 3,100 combat missions. Eight aircraft were lost, and one pilot, Navy Lieutenant Michael Scott Speicher, was killed. Speicher was flying an F/A-18 Hornet of Strike Fighter Squadron 81 (VFA-81) off the aircraft carrier USS *Saratoga*. He was shot down about 100 miles west of Baghdad, but the actual circumstances of his death were unclear. Years later, after his classification had been "missing in action", his remains were discovered in the desert. Although early reports suggested that the F/A-18 was shot down by a surface-to-air missile, later indications pointed to an air-launched

R-40 missile fired from an Iraqi MiG-25 fighter. Speicher is widely acknowledged as the first American combat casualty of the Gulf War.

The phased air war made steady progress in its multiple objectives, and one land-based Marine A-6E Intruder pilot explained the early period. "The first week of the war, called Phase I, involved softening up defensive sites, bridges, airfields, some road systems, and power plants. These were up north. For the first few days of the air war, we dealt primarily with Baghdad and Basra – and all the area in between. We were based out of Bahrain, so it takes 20 minutes till you go 'feet dry' to the land, right on up to the target area. We were under heavy triple-A for 20 minutes. Everywhere you looked, there was fire coming up at you. Once you released your bombs and left the target area, it seemed like an eternity before you returned to base. In addition, there were numerous SAMs."

Although Iraqi fighter operations were substantially suppressed, when enemy aircraft ventured into the skies, the air-to-air combat was one-sided. Among the first Coalition pilots to claim a victory against an Iraqi plane, Air Force Captain Steve Tate shot down a Mirage F-1 while leading a flight of four F-15Cs carrying out escort duty for strike aircraft in the vicinity of Baghdad. At first, the enemy fighter appeared to be a SAM launched at his formation.

"My number three had just turned south, and I was headed northeast," he said in a post-mission interview. "I don't know if the bogey was after him. I locked him up, confirmed he was hostile, and fired a missile. When the plane exploded, the whole sky lit up. It burned all the way to the ground then blew up. After identifying a hostile aircraft about 12 miles away, I just let FOX-1 (Sparrow air-to-air missile) go. Then about four miles in front of me I get a huge fireball."

In multiple engagements, the F-15 provided support to the opposing Soviet aircraft types. Captain Ayedh al-Shamrani of the Royal Saudi Air Force claimed two Iraqi Mirage F-1s while flying an F-15 near the Kuwaiti border. Two

American F-15 pilots shot down two enemy MiG-21s and two Su-25 attack planes in one air engagement, while another tandem of Eagle pilots dispatched three MiG-23 fighters and another Mirage F-1. An estimated 42 Iraqi planes were shot down in aerial combat, and dozens more were destroyed on the ground before the remainder of Saddam Hussein's air force sought sanctuary in Iran. Altogether, Iraqi aircraft losses were estimated at more than 400 planes.

RAF Tornado pilots successfully dropped specialised JP-233 cluster bombs on Iraqi runways, braving torrents of anti-aircraft fire. French Mirage 2000 fighters flew more than 600 missions, some of them aimed at munitions storage facilities in Kuwait, and Italian pilots flew 226 sorties against Iraqi targets.

When the success of Phase I was apparent, the air war shifted through additional strategic and tactical operations. One strike pilot described his role: "Our standard load for Phase I was laser-guided bombs and the 2,000lb iron bombs. Phases II and III were the softening up ones, and Phase IV was the ground war. So, we switched to Mk-82 iron bombs and Mk-20 Rockeye, carrying between 12 to 16 each. And we always carried at least one laser-guided bomb. If we found a decent target and needed pinpoint accuracy, we had it on hand."

As the air war progressed, the tally of destruction was immense. General Horner received intelligence that approximately 100,000 Iraqi personnel had been killed, wounded, or surrendered as a result of air attacks. Meanwhile, tactical aircraft continued to pummel enemy armour, strongpoints, and troop and supply concentrations that were visible to the naked eye or detected through the smoke and debris of war as smart munitions penetrated the veil. One highly visible example of Coalition tactical air strength was the A-10 Thunderbolt ground attack plane, flying low and slow over targets and devastating exposed enemy tanks with a 30mm nose cannon firing shells of depleted uranium and Maverick guided missiles. The A-10

US Navy Lieutenant Michael Scott Speicher was killed when his F/A-18 Hornet was shot down on the first night of the air campaign. *(US Government via Wikimedia Commons)*

The Lockheed F-117 Nighthawk stealth attack aircraft completed many missions over Baghdad. *(US Government via Wikimedia Commons)*

Camouflaged against the desert floor, an Italian Air Force Tornado flies during Desert Storm. *(Italian Ministry of Defence via Wikimedia Commons)*

A Tornado strike aircraft of the Royal Saudi Air Force prepares for take-off.
(US Government via Wikimedia Commons)

in Iraqi secret police headquarters. Both were coerced into reading bogus statements that they later repudiated, condemning Coalition aggression. The prisoners were repatriated under the terms of the Gulf War ceasefire.

The success of the Coalition air offensive against Saddam Hussein and the Iraqi army cannot be overstated. It was the mightiest assemblage of air power and leading-edge technology the world had ever seen, combined with the heroism and determination of aircrews from numerous nations to damage or destroy much of the enemy's combat capability. While it may be considered that air power alone could at some point have compelled an Iraqi withdrawal from Kuwait, the campaign did succeed handsomely in paving the way for the ground component of Desert Storm to yield the final victory. ■

was remarkably survivable as several took heavy punishment from enemy anti-aircraft fire and managed to bring their pilots home.

Inevitably, though, there were losses. During the air war the Coalition lost 75 aircraft, including 52 fixed wing and 23 helicopters. In the course of Desert Storm, 46 Coalition airmen were either killed or listed as missing in action. Sources vary as to the number captured by the Iraqis, one listing up to ten individuals: six Americans, a single Kuwaiti, an Italian, and two British. These prisoners were used by Iraqi authorities in the ongoing propaganda war, paraded before glaring lights and television cameras.

One captured pilot, British Flight Lieutenant John Peters was visibly injured when he was shown to the world via television alongside his Navigator John Nichol. Their Tornado had been shot down at an altitude of just 50ft over Ar Rumaylah Southwest Air Base, and he had apparently been beaten by his captors. US Navy pilot Jeffrey Zaun was blindfolded, handcuffed, and held in solitary confinement in a dark cell

Destroyed by Coalition forces during the Gulf War, an Iraqi MiG-29 fighter lies a burnt ruin.
(US Army via Wikimedia Commons)

ATTACK AT
KHAFJI

Captured at the Battle of Khafji, this Iraqi T-55 tank is now on display at the Tank Museum, Bovington. *(Creative Commons Hohum via Wikimedia Commons)*

IRONICALLY, THE FIRST ground action of any significance in the Gulf War was initiated by the Iraqi army at the direction of Saddam Hussein. Perhaps the Iraqi leader felt compelled to respond to the pummelling his forces had received from Coalition air power, to make some statement that his army possessed the will and the means to continue to resist.

The Iraqi offensive action, characterised more as probing attacks by Coalition commanders, began on January 29, 1991, and concluded three days later in defeat. Crossing the frontier with Saudi Arabia, the Iraqis occupied the Saudi border town of Khafji, and a pitched battle for its possession raged for hours. Four days prior to the Iraqi incursion, Saddam Hussein had met in Basra with senior officers to set his plan in motion. Three divisions of the Iraqi III and IV Corps, the 1st and 5th Mechanized and the 3rd Armoured, led the assault, which was launched at four separate penetration points. Some observers have theorised that the Iraqi objectives were to inflict casualties on the Coalition forces, take prisoners for use as bargaining chips in future negotiations, and even to seize the oil fields at Dammam more than 500 miles inside Saudi territory.

On the night of January 29, four Iraqi battalions, roughly 2,000 troops and 80 tanks, advanced during operations along a 50-mile stretch of the front lines. Although the attackers achieved initial surprise, their early movements had not gone undetected, generating air attacks and exchanges of artillery and rocket fire. When the Iraqi advance grew in strength, orders were issued to Coalition forward reconnaissance and observation elements to temporarily pull back. Responding to the warnings issued from forward positions, aircraft, including the Marine AH-1 Cobra gunship helicopters and fixed-wing A-6 Intruder, A-10 Thunderbolt, AC-130 gunships, and Harrier jump jet attack aircraft, flew numerous combat sorties. The air assets struck a heavy blow against some of the invading armoured columns, although visibility was poor.

While the Iraqi thrusts were generally repelled early on, one column managed to reach Khafji after absorbing significant losses from the air response. Just after midnight on January 30, the first Iraqi vehicles entered the empty town, startling US Army personnel in two trucks engaged in a routine supply delivery. One truck managed to escape, but the other crashed, its two occupants taken prisoner. At first, an all-out air assault was considered as the best means of forcing the Iraqis out of Khafji, but this option was soon discounted due to the presence of buildings that would require dangerously close approaches by the planes in order to identify and attack enemy targets.

Meanwhile, Radio Baghdad took full advantage of what amounted to a propaganda coup. "Oh Iraqis! Oh Arabs! Oh Muslims who believe in justice! Your faithful and courageous ground forces have moved to teach the aggressors the lessons they deserve!"

Subsequently, in joint consultation with General Khaled bin Sultan, commander of Saudi ground forces, Coalition commander General Norman Schwarzkopf authorised a ground operation to retake Khafji. The resources close at hand included

This US Marine Humvee vehicle was hit by Iraqi small arms fire during the Battle of Khafji. *(Creative Commons Richard Lovell via Wikimedia Commons)*

This view of the Saudi town of Khafji was taken before the Iraqi incursion that turned it into a battlefield. *(US Navy via Wikimedia Commons)*

Twisted, blackened metal is all that remains of a US Marine LAV-25 hit by friendly fire at Khafji. *(US Navy via Wikimedia Commons)*

Pieces of blasted armour lie surrounding a destroyed Iraqi tank at Khafji. *(Government of Iraq via Wikimedia Commons)*

commander was tactically indecisive, while battalion officers were waiting for orders. Marine advisors were attached to the Saudi units, along with elements of the 3rd Marine Regiment, and movement to the north and west of the town was undertaken to cut off any Iraqi reinforcements and prevent those inside Khafji from retreating. The Qataris moved seven French-built AMX-30 tanks up to support the Saudi 2nd Battalion. Along with Saudi M-60 tanks moving eastwards, these armoured forces prevented any Iraqi tanks from reaching the town.

Artillery of the 10th Marine Regiment opened fire on the Iraqis and was joined by Saudi M-109 155mm self-propelled howitzers in the bombardment. One Marine officer related: "The first two days, Marine artillery supported us. However, the Saudis insisted it was their sector and their responsibility, so they wanted to fire their artillery. They would hit the target all right, but when we asked them to cease fire, they would

the 2nd Brigade, 7th Battalion of the Saudi National Guard, two companies of Qatari tanks, and supporting US Marine and Army personnel, mainly reconnaissance and special forces respectively.

When the Iraqis reached Khafji, two Marine reconnaissance teams from the 1st Division found themselves trapped in the town. They hid almost in plain sight, holed up in a four-storey apartment building. Surrounded by hostile soldiers, they performed admirably, sending coded radio messages that vectored in air strikes and pinpointed targets for incoming Coalition artillery. During their 36-hour ordeal, these 12 Marines remained undetected. One close call occurred when Iraqi soldiers entered the building, searched the first floor, but declined to climb the stairs. The Marines were hidden on the roof ready to detonate anti-personnel Claymore mines after burning their code books.

One Marine remembered: "We could see their heads bobbing up and down. They sure would have had a rude awakening if they had come up after us." Another American recalled: "I'd be lying if I didn't say that dying had crossed my mind. We were shaking for two days from cold and fear."

The initial counterattack at Khafji took shape in a rather haphazard manner. The Saudi brigade

Artillerymen of the 10th Marine Regiment set their M198 155mm howitzer up to fire at the enemy in Khafji. *(US Marine Corps via Wikimedia Commons)*

In this painting titled *Cleaning Up Khafji*, Marines of the 3rd Battalion, 3rd Regiment are shown in the rubble of the town. *(US Marine Corps via Wikimedia Commons)*

(anti-tank missiles) were outdistancing the Iraqi weapons systems by 2,000 metres. By midday, we were tightening the ring on the Iraqis in Khafji. There was less and less chance for us to use close air support because we were fighting in close quarters. However, the fast movers were really accurate with their 20mm cannons."

Saudi infantry moved up from the south joined by the heavy gun sections of the 3rd Marine Regiment and the Qataris in reserve. Preliminary fire was laid down by the 1st Battalion, 12th Marines. The attack went in at approximately 8.30am, and three Saudi armoured cars were disabled by Iraqi rocket-propelled grenades. More than a dozen Iraqi tanks and armoured personnel carriers were destroyed, six other vehicles captured, and over 100 enemy prisoners taken. The Saudis took four casualties, two of them killed in action. The Saudi 7th and 8th Battalions linked up and drove the Iraqis from

send in another barrage... I must say the forward observer was invaluable. He did a great job."

The first day's fighting saw some gains by the Saudi ground troops, but their main assault towards Khafji was stymied. Iraqi tanks attacked south of the town and lost three T-55s in action against the Qatari AMX-30s. After losing an armoured car to enemy fire, the Saudis brought up reinforcements and their 5th Battalion, 2nd Brigade joined the effort in the north to block

any Iraqi reinforcements. Within hours, further Saudi troops fed into the fight gained ground late in the day, but concerns surrounding friendly fire caused them to fall back the following morning after capturing scores of Iraqi prisoners.

On January 31, the second day of the Battle of Khafji, the Coalition attacks gained momentum. "...The Saudis fought much better," said one Marine. "They found that their M-60s outgunned the T-55 by 900 metres or so and the TOWs

Graffiti scrawled on its hull, this Iraqi T-55 tank was knocked out in the fighting around Khafji. *(Government of Iraq via Wikimedia Commons)*

Two Iraqi tanks, a T-55 and a Chinese-built T-69, appear to have rammed one another in the confusion of battle. *(Government of Iraq via Wikimedia Commons)*

General Khalid bin Sultan commanded Saudi forces in Desert Storm and directed operations around Khafji. *(US Army via Wikimedia Commons)*

the southern section of the town. By 6.30pm, the 7th Battalion had withdrawn to reprovision, while the 8th remained in Khafji. Simultaneously, the Qatari tank companies leveraged Marine artillery support to skirt northwards and guard against further enemy incursions.

"Funny thing," mused one Marine. "The Saudis don't clear a house like we do. If they're walking down the street and they take fire from a house, they blow it up. Crude, but effective I guess."

As the battle for Khafji reached its zenith, an Iraqi amphibious force came to grief. Intending to land on the coast and disgorge soldiers to rush towards the town, the enemy watercraft were spotted in the open and virtually annihilated in the Persian Gulf. Two companies of Iraqi infantry with about 20 armoured vehicles remained in Khafji overnight, but the Saudis destroyed the remaining organised resistance, systematically reducing sporadic hot spots throughout the day on February 1.

While the streets of Khafji were being cleared, Coalition aircraft fired on targets of opportunity and inflicted some friendly casualties. One Marine Harrier pilot recalled an engagement on the last day of the battle. "As the Iraqis were trying to flee Khafji, we hit a couple of the retreating columns. That area looked like a moonscape. When we went north to confront them, we went nose to nose. I dropped Rockeye [air-launched cluster bombs] on them and egressed back to the south and west."

In the closing hours of the melee, one significant incident of friendly fire occurred when an American aircraft fired missiles at a group of eight Marine LAV-25 light armoured reconnaissance vehicles, mistaking them for Iraqi Soviet-made BTR-60s. One LAV-25 was struck, killing eight Marines.

Coalition casualties totalled 43 killed, 25 of them American. Fourteen of the fatalities occurred on January 31 when an AC-130 gunship was shot down by an Iraqi surface-to-air missile. Eighteen Saudi soldiers were killed and 50 wounded. The Marines lost three LAV-25 vehicles, while the Saudis lost ten armoured cars and two tanks,

one of them struck by a 100mm round from an Iraqi T-55. Nearly 1,000 Iraqi soldiers were listed as casualties, 71 of them killed, although US estimates of the enemy dead neared 300.

As the remnants of the Iraqi forces aimed at Khafji melted away, Saddam Hussein clung to the notion that the battle had been an Iraqi victory, yet the harsh reality was apparent. Coalition forces had demonstrated their capacity to utilise air power to complement ground troops, while artillery had been timely and accurate.

When the battle died down, the Coalition had regained the initiative in Desert Storm, but three more weeks would elapse before its war machine unleashed its full pent-up fury. ■

A US Marine LAV-25 light armoured vehicle fires its main 25mm cannon. A LAV-25 was destroyed by friendly fire at Khafji. *(US Government via Wikimedia Commons)*

An AC-130 gunship similar to this example was shot down by an Iraqi surface-to-air missile during the Battle of Khafji. *(US Air Force via Wikimedia Commons)*

GRAND STRATEGY – THE HAIL MARY

IT WAS A lethal combination of strength and deception. Following the five-week aerial campaign that pounded Iraqi forces and eroded the morale of their troops, destroyed many tanks and artillery and other weapons that might resist, and degraded Saddam Hussein's combat efficiency, General Norman Schwarzkopf unleashed the 100-hour ground war against the Iraqi army. Its success was almost immediate, and its progress dazzled the world.

While the air campaign progressed, Schwarzkopf had conferred with Coalition military partners and discussed the coming ground offensive with General Colin Powell, Chairman of the Joint Chiefs of Staff. Without compromising security, Powell described what was to come in response to a reporter's question. The general succinctly replied: "Our strategy to go after this army is very, very simple. First, we're going to cut it off, and then we're going to kill it."

Putting his grand strategy into motion, Schwarzkopf intended to fix and hold Iraqi attention in the frontier between occupied Kuwait and Saudi Arabia. Marines were to take up stations off the Kuwaiti coast to convince the enemy that an amphibious assault might be imminent, and 17,000 combat troops of the 4th Marine Expeditionary Brigade aboard 31 ships did just that, training and drilling while the Iraqis watched. At the same time, Schwarzkopf secretly shifted the main thrust of what would be called Operation Desert

Coalition forces destroyed hundreds of Iraqi T-55 tanks like this example abandoned near Kuwait City. *(US Navy via Wikimedia Commons)*

Sabre to the west and prepared to launch the ground phase of Desert Storm, which commenced on February 24, 1991, or 'G-Day'.

A veil of secrecy shrouded the movement westward that began on February 14. The XVIII Airborne Corps and the VII Corps moved over 200,000 troops, air assets, tanks, and artillery to the Iraqi frontier, and the weight of the 'Hail Mary' or 'Left Hook' was in place. The intent was to complete a wide flanking movement that would bypass Iraqi defensive concentrations and then cut off the retreat of enemy forces compelled to withdraw from Kuwait. In the process, the VII Corps was expected to engage and thoroughly defeat the best Iraqi divisions, those of the elite Republican Guard.

Meanwhile, the 1st and 2nd Marine Divisions, along with Egyptian, Saudi, Syrian, Moroccan, Qatari, and Kuwaiti troops, maintained positions opposite the so-called Saddam Line,

M1A1 Abrams main battle tanks of the US 3rd Armored Division slash across the Iraqi desert. *(US Navy via Wikimedia Commons)*

A US Marine M-60 tank utilising a bulldozer blade breaches the Saddam Line on February 24, 1991. *(US Department of Defense via Wikimedia Commons)*

Fires rage after Iraqis set Kuwaiti oil fields ablaze with the approach of Coalition forces. *(US Department of Defense via Wikimedia Commons)*

a well-designed but ultimately poorly defended series of bunkers, berms, artillery emplacements, minefields, barbed wire, and even ditches filled with oil to be set aflame to retard a Coalition advance. Special operations insertions into Iraq had taken place in the weeks preceding the ground war, and their clandestine missions were ongoing. All the while, the possibility of Iraqi retaliation with chemical weapons was a primary concern, and Coalition forces were outfitted with appropriate gear to survive such an eventuality.

In the pre-dawn hours of February 24, Coalition forces began their attacks. In the west, the XVIII Airborne Corps, including the 82nd and 101st Airborne Divisions, along with the French 6th Light Armoured Division and the US 24th Division (Mechanized), advanced north into Iraq and secured the western flank of the Coalition offensive. The French seized their initial objective, a cluster of Iraqi fortifications nicknamed 'Rochambeau', and swiftly advanced to capture the city of Al Salman, 95 miles deep inside Iraq, along with its nearby airfield. These initial operations were furthered by the 101st Airborne utilising 300 helicopters to insert 2,000 troops 70 miles inside enemy territory along the Euphrates River, to establish a refuelling base for rotary aircraft. The 101st also conducted further air assault penetrations deep inside Iraq beyond G-Day. By nightfall on February 25, the XVIII Airborne Corps had defeated the Iraqi 45th Division and taken 2,900 prisoners in the process. The vital highway near the city of Nasiriya was also secured.

The thrust of XVIII Airborne Corps was so rapid that Schwarzkopf ordered VII Corps to advance earlier than previously scheduled from its positions west of Wadi al-Batin. Little resistance was encountered in the beginning, and by the third day of the offensive, the VII Corps turned northeast to take on the Republican Guard directly. Along the Saddam Line, the 1st and 2nd Marine Divisions and the Tiger

A soldier of the 101st Airborne Division cleans his rifle just before the commencement of the ground phase of Desert Storm. *(US Government via Wikimedia Commons)*

Two AMX-30 main battle tanks of the French 6th Light Armoured Division pause outside the Iraqi town of Al Salman, Iraq. *(US Department of Defense via Wikimedia Commons)*

Brigade of the US Army's 2nd Armored Division advanced into Kuwait, along with forces from the Arab nations. Although resistance to the initial thrust was heavier than elsewhere, the Marines and accompanying Coalition forces reached the outskirts of Kuwait City swiftly and scooped up thousands of demoralised and dazed Iraqi soldiers, many of them offering only token resistance before surrendering.

By the fourth day of Operation Desert Sabre, all Coalition objectives had been achieved. Kuwait City was liberated. The Republican Guard had been ravaged, and a cease-fire was soon enacted.

With the 2nd Marine Division on his left flank, General James Michael Myatt, commanding the

US Marines of Task Force Ripper lace up new boots before breaching the Saddam Line and plunging into Kuwait. *(US Government via Wikimedia Commons)*

Combat engineers work with tanks equipped with mine rakes as they are positioned to breach the Saddam Line. *(US Department of Defense via Wikimedia Commons)*

1st Marine Division, organised four specialised task forces, Taro, Grizzly, Ripper, and Papa Bear, to execute the assault on the Saddam Line. These consisted of light armoured vehicles, artillery, and M-60 tanks supported by helicopter units with troop transport capability for flank support. On the day before the offensive, one observer took stock of the territory that had to be crossed. "A 12ft-high berm had been bulldozed the entire length of the Kuwait border by the Iraqis, and we were behind it," he recalled. "The sky over Kuwait on the other side was pitch black from our aerial bombardment and the burning oil fields."

Colonel Carl Fulford commanded Task Force Ripper and related: "The initial breach was relatively undefended with only a small skirmish on our left flank. Both Grizzly and Taro had done a good job of eliminating any organised resistance on Ripper's flanks. We did lose one M-60 tank to a double impulse mine. Fortunately,

General James Michael Myatt commanded the 1st Marine Division through the ground war in Desert Storm. *(Creative Commons Lai345 via Wikimedia Commons)*

no-one was injured and we completed crossing four breaches in one and one-half hours. At the second obstacle belt, we were getting some incoming artillery along our front. However, it wasn't very accurate nor was it sustained which surprised me… Counterbattery was effective, but I think the air war had destroyed their command-and-control capabilities so that every time a plane went overhead, it put the fear of God in them. They probably pulled the lanyard and ran."

As the first day ended, the Marines had eliminated approximately three Iraqi divisions. During the night that followed, the rapid advance of the Marines and Arab forces into Kuwait, the Iraqis set fire to the Burgan and Al Gudair oil fields, sending flames and billowing black smoke skywards. However, the rapidity of the ground offensive into Kuwait was not slowed. With the pace exceeding expectations, Schwarzkopf extended the distance of some forces in their penetration and later their

turn to the east towards Kuwait City. By the morning of February 27, Task Force Ripper was fighting its way to Kuwait International Airport and engaged a large Iraqi armoured force. In the swirl of the battle, the Marine M-60s and TOW anti-tank missiles destroyed more than 100 Iraqi vehicles, including 60 tanks.

By February 28, with the Marine vanguard halted on the outskirts of Kuwait City and the airport secured, Arab forces moved into the capital and linked up with Kuwaiti resistance fighters and US Navy SEALs that infiltrated during the execution of the amphibious feint two days earlier. The Marines that followed recalled a tumultuous scene as crowds celebrated in the streets, waving American and Kuwaiti flags.

Meanwhile, as the Marines captured the airport and sought to cut off the escape of Iraqi forces fleeing Kuwait City, elements of the Tiger Brigade occupied high ground to the northwest at Al-Mutla Ridge in a commanding position

An M1A1 Abrams main battle tank sits under camouflage netting just prior to the opening ground assault of Desert Storm. The ground phase of Desert Storm was designated Operation Desert Sabre. *(US National Archives and Records Administration via Wikimedia Commons)*

for miles. Co-ordinating with air strikes, the Tiger Brigade rained destruction on Iraqi forces fleeing the area. The road soon became known around the world as the 'Highway of Death'.

In the west, the success of the French 6th Armoured Division and the US Airborne divisions allowed the 24th Infantry (Mechanized) to jump off five hours earlier than expected. Advancing at incredible speeds up to 30mph, the 24th sliced 75 miles into Iraq by the end of the first day. The rapid movement of all Coalition forces in the region prevented the Iraqis from reinforcing their troops to the south from Baghdad. Control

of airfields and highways was accomplished with the 3rd Brigade, 101st Airborne making the longest air assault combat advance in history, 175 miles to the banks of the Euphrates. Moving north and then northeast, the 24th Division brushed aside light opposition and claimed thousands of prisoners. Within hours, these combined forces were conducting raids against Iraqi supply caches and establishing lodgements on the far side of the river.

With its western flank being secured and the direct drive through the Saddam Line underway, VII Corps, including the US 1st, 2nd, and 3rd Armoured Divisions, the British 1st Armoured Division, and the US 1st Infantry Division, 1st Cavalry Division, and 2nd Armored Cavalry Regiment, executed the 'Left Hook' or 'Hail Mary' that sprung Schwarzkopf's trap of the Republican Guard.

The elite Iraqi divisions were still awaiting orders to move south, where the attention of their crippled command-and-control were focused, when the Republican Guard came under attack from the leading edge of VII Corps. Fifteen hours ahead of schedule, the Coalition sledgehammer had crossed into Iraq about 70 miles west of the border between Saudi Arabia and Kuwait, first attacking parallel to the XVIII Airborne Corps and then swinging to the east. The 1st Infantry Division led the way, taking thousands of prisoners almost immediately. The 1st Cavalry Division attacked to the left, while the 2nd Armored Cavalry Regiment bowled forward on the right with the 1st and 3rd Armored Divisions in its wake. The British 1st Armoured Division followed the 1st Infantry Division, and by the time these Americans stepped off, the 1st and 3rd Armored Divisions were already 18 miles inside Iraq.

On the second day of Desert Sabre, VII Corps continued its northward advance to

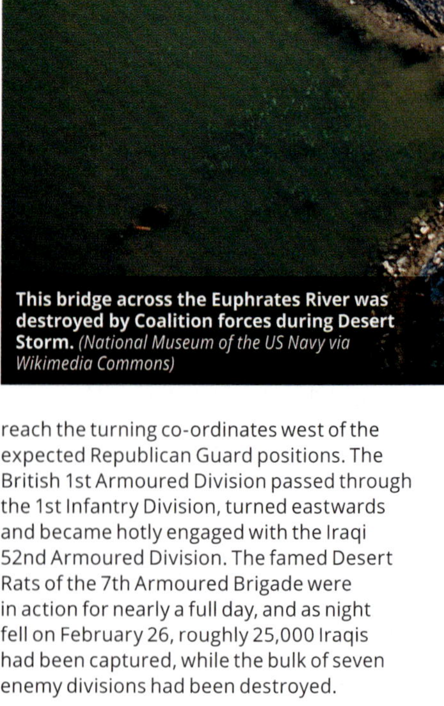

This bridge across the Euphrates River was destroyed by Coalition forces during Desert Storm. *(National Museum of the US Navy via Wikimedia Commons)*

reach the turning co-ordinates west of the expected Republican Guard positions. The British 1st Armoured Division passed through the 1st Infantry Division, turned eastwards and became hotly engaged with the Iraqi 52nd Armoured Division. The famed Desert Rats of the 7th Armoured Brigade were in action for nearly a full day, and as night fell on February 26, roughly 25,000 Iraqis had been captured, while the bulk of seven enemy divisions had been destroyed.

Soldiers examine this Chinese-built Type 69 tank destroyed by the French 6th Light Armoured Division in the western area of Desert Storm operations. *(US Air Force via Wikimedia Commons)*

Tanks of the US Army roll past a burning Iraqi tank during Operation Desert Sabre. *(US Department of Defense via Wikimedia Commons)*

havoc with the Iraqi 12th Armored Division and Tawakalna Division of the Republican Guard.

During the last hours of the ground war on February 27-28, elements of VII Corps fought the huge tank battles at Medina Ridge and Norfolk. Republican Guard forces were engaged and systematically decimated wherever they were found. When the cessation of hostilities was ordered, the VII Corps was continuing its relentless eastward advance.

Clearly, the Iraqi army had been defeated in battle. Continuing the Coalition onslaught would, some military officers believed, produce little in return. The enemy might lose more men and a relative few more tanks, but that was only a limited return for the risk. Coalition casualties had been light, and the prospect of sustaining more killed or wounded was simply unreasonable.

After a detailed briefing on the situation, President Bush was convinced that the objectives of Desert Storm had been achieved, including the ejection of the Iraqis from Kuwait, control of the air and of lines of communication, the securing of Kuwait International Airport, the outflanking and destruction of the Republican Guard, and the liberation of Kuwait City. At 9pm Eastern Standard Time (on February 27), he addressed the nation.

"Kuwait is liberated. Iraq's army is defeated," Bush declared. "…I am pleased to announce that at midnight Eastern Standard Time, exactly 100 hours since ground operations commenced and six weeks since the start of Desert Storm, all United States and Coalition forces will suspend offensive combat operations." ∎

Tanks and armoured personnel carriers of the 3rd Marine Division prepare to move forward as the ground war gets underway. *(US Navy via Wikimedia Commons)*

When VII Corps completed its eastward turn the following day, its onslaught continued. Some of the best units in the Iraqi army were engaged as the 3rd Armored Division moved forwards in the centre, the 1st Armored Division on the left, and the 2nd Armored Cavalry Regiment and 1st Infantry Division on the right. The British 1st Armoured Division was in step to the south. As the day wore on, the vastly outnumbered 2nd Armored Cavalry Regiment fought the great Battle of 73 Easting, wreaking

British soldiers of the 1st Armoured Division pause with their Challenger 1 tank during operations along the highway between Kuwait City and Basra, Iraq. *(US Army via Wikimedia Commons)*

An Iraqi tank, a Chinese-built Type 69 derived from the Soviet-era T-62, burns after being destroyed during the Gulf War. *(US Navy via Wikimedia Commons)*

BATTLE OF 73 EASTING

THE DESERT WAS barren, and the location had previously been identified only as a Universal Transverse Mercator line in the trackless expanse. By the end of Operation Desert Sabre, the ground component of Operation Desert Storm, 73 Easting would be famous across the globe.

Five Troops, E (Eagle), F (Fox), G (Ghost), I (Iron), and K (Killer), of the US Army's 2nd Armored Cavalry Regiment (ACR), the literal tip of the spear as the VII Corps penetrated Iraqi defences and raced to engage the vaunted Republican Guard, fought a sharp but ultimately one-sided battle against the enemy, on February 26-27, 1991.

The Battle of 73 Easting shaped up somewhat by accident as the stated mission of the cavalry elements was to scout ahead of the heavy combat units of VII Corps. Although each troop was a compact, efficient fighting force in itself, with nine superb M1A1 Abrams tanks, 12 M3 Bradley Cavalry Fighting Vehicles, a pair of fire support 120mm mortars, and 130 highly trained soldiers, they were directed to leave the toughest fighting to the bulk of VII Corps.

A preparatory air campaign had effectively blinded the Iraqi high command to Coalition force movements, while a campaign of deception, including amphibious manoeuvres, fake radio traffic, and special operations endeavours had worked to degrade enemy combat effectiveness and prompt the Iraqi senior commanders to orient the majority of their armour and infantry to the south to guard against supposed landings on the Kuwaiti coast. Meanwhile, the wide envelopment of the 'Hail Mary' flanking movement was executed flawlessly by the XVIII Airborne Corps, and the VII Corps jumped off from its bases in Saudi Arabia to cut off

This Iraqi tank was blasted by Coalition forces in the swirl of the Battle of 73 Easting. *(US Army via Wikimedia Commons)*

This M3 Bradley Cavalry Fighting Vehicle was destroyed during the opening moments of the Battle of 73 Easting. *(US Army via Wikimedia Commons)*

the retreat of Iraqi forces once they realised that a deadly threat existed to their rear.

The advance of VII Corps electrified the world in a tremendous display of firepower and manoeuvre that set a remarkable standard for modern ground warfare. Along the way, its 100-hours of offensive operations were marked by pitched encounters with Iraqi T-72, T-62, and T-55 tanks, as well as BMP infantry fighting vehicles, all Soviet-built,

This distant photo depicts destroyed Iraqi tanks and armoured vehicles, along with abandoned strongpoints captured during the Battle of 73 Easting. *(Creative Commons Fury 1991 via Wikimedia Commons)*

that were manned by the Republican Guard and other formations of the Iraqi army.

By February 26, the Iraqis had become aware of the envelopment threat and turned the Republican Guard Tawakalna Mechanized Division west to confront VII Corps. The second day of Desert Sabre would prove momentous as the 2nd Armored Cavalry Regiment ranged ahead of VII Corps, searching for the enemy.

The initial brush with Iraqi forces had come in the gathering darkness of February 24, not long after Desert Sabre commenced. Penetrating about 20km into the Iraqi lines, the Americans ran into troops and armoured vehicles that resisted. These were subdued by rapid fire from the M3 Bradley 25mm cannon and TOW anti-tank missiles. Mortar rounds arced into enemy positions, and soon Fox Troop was rounding up scores of prisoners.

Hours later, Ghost Troop wiped out an Iraqi reconnaissance detachment, dispatching its 12 vehicles, and confirmed that the Republican Guard was nearby via interrogation,s and other intelligence, gleaned from the short firefight. Orders were then received to begin the planned turn to a northeastern axis of advance from the earlier northward penetration.

A night of heavy rains preceded an encounter with elements of the Iraqi 50th Brigade. Several companies of enemy troops and vehicles were neutralised, and on February 26 the armoured cavalrymen received orders to adjust their operational sector in co-operation with the British 1st Armoured Division to the south. While executing the corresponding manoeuvre, the 2nd Armored Cavalry destroyed an Iraqi tank.

By late morning, a strong sandstorm swirled around the 2nd ACR in the vicinity of 60 Easting. Still, the weather did not deter its aggressiveness in blasting elements of the Tawakalna Division. When the fighting subsided around noon, the cavalrymen reported the destruction of 25 armoured personnel carriers, 23 T-55 tanks, and numerous other vehicles.

The VII Corps was also on the move, and the 2nd ACR was subsequently ordered to advance to 70 Easting but to avoid initiating a general engagement with the Republican Guard – that was the job of the four armoured and mechanised divisions to its rear. Three cavalry squadrons moved ahead, eight of the regiment's nine troops abreast. The troops of 2nd Squadron (Cougar Squadron) were deployed in wedge formations, and Captain HR McMaster, commanding Eagle Troop, unknowingly entered the grounds of an Iraqi training facility with a road running parallel to their route of advance, in and out of a small village, and then to the Kuwaiti frontier.

McMaster later reported that the enemy had utilised the reverse slope of a long ridge for defensive positions, expecting that attacking American tanks might expose their undersides to counter fire as they crested the high ground. Reportedly, the Iraqi commander was a Major Mohammed, who is believed to have received some training in defensive deployment in the United States. He placed anti-aircraft guns to be used against the American armour and machine gun nests along the road and in the village, while mines had been sown, and bunkers and anti-tank ditches blocked the way forward. McMaster noted that about 40 T-72s and 16 BMPs were dug in roughly 1,000yds beyond the ridge. The Iraqi command post was about 3,000yds further east, where Mohammed had stationed 18 T-72s in reserve, along with other armoured vehicles.

McMaster would later rise to the rank of lieutenant general and serve as national security advisor during the first administration of President Donald Trump. But that was in the future – the business at hand in February 1991 was deadly serious.

Eagle Troop approached 67 Easting – just short of its furthest line of authorised advance – but fighting broke out and quickly escalated. "Staff Sergeant John McReynolds' Bradley drove atop an Iraqi bunker serving as an observation post," said McMaster, who was aboard his M1A1 nicknamed *Mad Max*. "Two

General McMaster, serving as national security advisor, sits to the left of President Trump during a 2017 meeting. *(US Government via Wikimedia Commons)*

Tanks of the US 3rd Armored Division, VII Corps move out during the opening hours of Operation Desert Storm. *(US Army via Wikimedia Commons)*

Iraqi armoured vehicles such as this 122mm self-propelled howitzer were dug in prior to the inception of Operation Desert Sabre. *(US Army via Wikimedia Commons)*

enemy soldiers emerged and surrendered, and McReynolds took them to the rear. The Bradley of McReynolds' wingman, Sergeant Maurice Harris, came under fire. As Harris engaged the enemy with his 25mm, 1st Lieutenant Tim Gauthier fired a TOW missile into the village so the explosion would orient our tanks. After my gunner, Staff Sergeant Craig Koch, fired a round to mark the target center, all nine tanks fired high explosive rounds into the village to suppress the enemy position."

When Harris radioed that his Bradley was being fired on, the response from his platoon leader was to the point. He tersely ordered:

"Well, kill them!" Eagle Troop and the bulk of 2nd Squadron were joined by 3rd Squadron, receiving clearance to roll ahead to 70 Easting. The fight was spreading to the south and east, but the cavalrymen had no way of knowing that they would soon be outnumbered at least three to one. As Eagle Troop shifted into a tanks-forward attack formation, one of its Bradleys took out another T-72 with a TOW missile. Seconds later, Sergeant Koch sounded an alarm: "Tanks direct front!"

From inside the turret of *Mad Max*, McMaster vividly recalled spotting eight T-72s dug in straight ahead. Koch, meanwhile, 'brewed

Shown with the rank of lieutenant general, HR McMaster led Eagle Troop as a young officer during the Battle of 73 Easting. *(US Army via Wikimedia Commons)*

up' two of the enemy tanks. Within seconds, all nine M1A1s were engaged. The darkness was torn by tongues of fire, and the captain noted that "everything within range was in flames". During a devastating blink of only eight seconds, Koch and *Mad Max* destroyed three Iraqi tanks. Altogether, the nine Abrams tanks of Eagle Troop accounted for 28 Iraqi tanks, 16 enemy armoured fighting vehicles and 30 trucks in less than a half hour of combat at 70 Easting. No American casualties were reported.

In the thick of the fight, Lieutenant John Gifford, executive officer aboard *Mad*

During the Iraq War, then-Colonel McMaster confers with officers of the 3rd Squadron, 1st Cavalry Regiment. *(US Army via Wikimedia Commons)*

Max, got Captain McMaster's attention on the radio. The message he delivered was not good news, but the Eagle Troop commander was committed to clearing the remainder of the Iraqi forces in the path of VII Corps. He could not simply disengage.

"I know you don't want to know this right now," Gifford advised, "but you're at the limit of advance; you're at the 70 Easting." McMaster paused for a moment and replied: "Tell them we can't stop. Tell them we're in contact, and we have to continue this attack. Tell them I'm sorry."

Once Eagle Troop and the rest of the 2nd ACR made contact with the Iraqis, they became entangled with a much larger force, and the escalation of the battle was beyond their control. The original plan to allow VII Corps to pass through and do the heavy fighting melted away temporarily in real-time combat. McMaster had no choice but to continue the battle. The risk involved in the situation was two-fold. The armoured cavalrymen might be

Iraqi Republican Guard troops abandoned this mobile surface-to-air missile launcher during Operation Desert Storm. *(US Department of Defense via Wikimedia Commons)*

In the wake of a nocturnal battle with Coalition armour, an Iraqi tank burns furiously. *(Creative Commons Fury 1991 via Wikimedia Commons)*

Retired Colonel Timothy Gauthier, a veteran of Eagle Troop, 2nd Armored Cavalry Regiment, cracks a bottle of champagne across a T-72 tank during ceremonies commemorating the 25th anniversary of the Battle of 73 Easting. *(US Army via Wikimedia Commons)*

This dug-in Iraqi armoured vehicle is pictured with thin camouflage netting for concealment. *(US Army via Wikimedia Commons)*

overwhelmed by the sheer numbers of Iraqi tanks and troops, and the road march formations of VII Corps might be prevented from deploying into combat wedges to come to the aid of the hard-pressed cavalry troops. Still, McMaster had no alternative but to press the attack, and he showed remarkable composure and presence of mind.

Eagle Troop was fully engaged with the 18th Mechanized Battalion of the Tawakalna Division, and the Battle of 73 Easting steadily expanded as other elements of the 2nd ACR continued their advance. The 1st and 3rd Troops of the 2nd ACR had already seen action the previous day when they 'roughed up' the Iraqi 50th Armored Brigade. They were still engaged with what was left of that enemy formation and taking on the 37th Brigade of the enemy 12th Armored Division south of the Tawakalna Division.

As the Abrams tanks and Bradley fighting vehicles moved ahead, a gap developed between the cavalry troops. Iron Troop, 3rd Squadron plugged the hole, while Ghost Troop, 2nd Squadron engaged the enemy north of Eagle Troop and Killer Troop, 3rd Squadron sought enemy armoured vehicles. The fighting continued through fading daylight and past sundown. Together, Iron Troop and Killer Troop destroyed 16 Iraqi tanks, and Iron Troop advanced from 70 Easting to take out an enemy command post. Meanwhile, McMaster ordered Eagle Troop to 73

An M1A1 Abrams main battle tank rolls forward raising a cloud of dust during Desert Storm. The Abrams played a key role in the Coalition ground victory. *(U.S. Government via Wikimedia Commons)*

Easting and reached the ridgeline where the Iraqi reserve tanks were located.

McMaster remembered: "My tank and others destroyed the first of the reserve from a range of approximately 1,000yds beginning at about 4.40pm. We could not see the others until we crested the rise and entered the assembly area. The enemy reserve was attempting to move out, but E Troop tanks destroyed all of them at close range before they could deploy."

Eagle Troop repelled sporadic infantry attacks and then blasted a thrust of enemy tanks and BMPs, taking the Iraqis under fire at extreme range and breaking up the concentration before it could engage. Accurate mortar and artillery fire hit

US soldiers inspect the wreckage of a Soviet-made BMP infantry fighting vehicle. *(US Department of Defense via Wikimedia Commons)*

Soldiers of the 2nd Armored Cavalry Regiment prepare for exercises in Germany in 2014. The regiment was heavily engaged at 73 Easting during the Gulf War. *(US Army via Wikimedia Commons)*

enemy command posts and rallying points, while infantrymen took out bunkers with satchel charges and hand grenades.

Ghost Troop occupied a ridgeline and fought off counterattacks by elements of the Tawakalna and 12th Armored Divisions for several hours. Enemy tanks supported by waves of infantry streamed towards the American positions, but timely air support and concentrated artillery boosted the defenders as the Iraqi advance was shattered. Ghost Troop destroyed two companies of enemy tanks, and scores of dead enemy soldiers were sprawled across the desert floor. During the sharp engagement, Ghost Troop fired more than half its available TOW missiles, while MLRS rocket systems and artillery fired more than 700 rounds. By 9pm, the enemy assault had shot its bolt.

Just after 10pm, leading elements of the 1st Infantry Division reached the forward positions of 3rd Squadron, 2nd ACR, south of Eagle Troop. By 2am on February 27, the 2nd ACR reached 74 Easting as the vanguard of VII Corps passed through the cavalry lines. The 1st Infantry Division brought with it six battalions of M1A1 tanks, more than 300 in total, along with heavy artillery in its advance towards the crossroads at Objective Norfolk.

In the Battle of 73 Easting, American forces suffered six killed and 19 wounded. Sergeant Nels Moller was killed by a shell fired from a BMP that was thought to have been eliminated. With other Bradley crewmen, he was attempting to clear its jammed 25mm cannon and restore its TOW launcher to working order at the time. The other casualties were caused primarily by friendly fire incidents. A single Bradley was lost to enemy action, and one M1A1 was slightly damaged by a mine.

In contrast, the 2nd Armored Cavalry Regiment destroyed two Iraqi armoured brigades, the 18th of the Tawakalna Division and the 37th of the 12th Armored Division. In the process, the Americans knocked out 159 Iraqi tanks and more than 250 other vehicles. More than 1,000 Iraqi soldiers were killed or wounded, and 2,000 taken prisoner.

The Battle of 73 Easting is remembered as one of the largest tank fights in the history of the US Army. It demonstrated superiority over Iraqi forces, while serving as a proving ground for Coalition forces as well trained, capably led, and equipped with superior land warfare systems and technology. ■

Eagle Troop veterans of the Battle of 73 Easting pose during the dedication of a monument to their courage. *(US Army via Wikimedia Commons)*

Sergeant Benjamin Hallford, a veteran of Fox Troop, 2nd Armored Cavalry Regiment, serves as master of ceremonies during anniversary observances of the Battle of 73 Easting. *(US Army via Wikimedia Commons)*

FIGHT AT MEDINA RIDGE

AFTER THE FIRING had died down, and the landscape was littered with burning Iraqi tanks and armoured personnel carriers, one American soldier, who had experienced combat aboard a Bradley fighting vehicle, caught his breath, and later declared: "I had never heard so many tank guns going off at the same time in my life, before or since. It was a pretty damn good fight." His was a real-time assessment of the sprawling Battle of Medina Ridge, which resulted in the destruction of the Medina Division of Saddam Hussein's Republican Guard.

February 27, 1991, was the decisive day of the Coalition ground offensive during the Gulf War. Executing General Norman Schwarzkopf's Hail Mary or Left Hook strategy, to cut off the escape of Iraqi forces attempting to retreat from Kuwait, the powerful VII Corps fought skirmishes and pitched battles at numerous locations. Although the combat was decidedly one-sided, and offensive operations concluded with a ceasefire after just 100 hours, there was uncertainty at times, and the resolve of the elite Iraqi Republican Guard to stand and give battle was confirmed.

On the same day that another decisive battle took place at Objective Norfolk to the west, the US 1st Armored Division, commanded by General Ron Griffith, along with the 3rd Brigade, 3rd Infantry Division, under Colonel James Riley, won a tremendous victory at Medina Ridge, just outside of the major Iraqi port city of Basra. The 1st Armored Division was a tremendous mailed fist with 348 superb M1A1 Abrams main battle tanks and a large complement of M2/M3 Bradley fighting vehicles. Altogether, its massive combat weight totalled 3,000 vehicles. In

General Ron Griffith led the 1st Armored Division that fought in the Battle of Medina Ridge. *(US Department of Defense via Wikimedia Commons)*

Shown with the rank of brigadier general, then Colonel James C Riley commanded the 3rd Brigade, 3rd Infantry Division, at Medina Ridge. *(US Department of Defense via Wikimedia Commons)*

company with the armored division, the infantry brigade was comprised of the 1st Squadron, 1st Cavalry Regiment, 1st and 4th Battalions, 7th Infantry Regiment, 2nd Battalion, 41st Field Artillery Regiment, and other attached units.

By the time the bulk of the 1st Armored Division reached the seven-mile-long rim of low-rising ground that would later be named Medina Ridge, its troops and tanks had fought elements of

three Iraqi divisions during their dash from Saudi Arabia and across the trackless desert, using global positioning system (GPS) data to remain oriented. Their opponents at Medina Ridge were the best the Iraqi army could field, highly trained and loyal to Saddam Hussein. The Medina Division of the Republican Guard included an estimated 400 Soviet-built T-62 and T-72 tanks, and the commander of the division, General Ayad

An M1A1 Abrams tank pauses in the desert during the 100-hour ground assault against Iraqi forces. *(U.S. Government via Wikimedia Commons)*

Futayyih Al-Rawi, had some understanding of battlefield armour tactics – but not enough.

A cavalry squadron of the 1st Armored Division made contact with the Iraqis before mid-day on the 27th, and reported the enemy positions amid overcast and rainy weather that was less than ideal for battle. Al-Rawi had decided to position his tanks on the reverse slope of the ridge, and such a defensive position did offer advantages, particularly in negating the greater range of the American tanks' and fighting vehicles' main cannon and lethal TOW anti-tank missiles. Further, the attackers would have to crest the ridge, momentarily exposing their more vulnerable undersides to Iraqi tank fire before they could bring their own guns to bear. However, the Iraqi commander made one fatal error, positioning his armour too far from the ridge.

In the event, the battle became a two-hour afternoon exercise in Iraqi attrition. The uneven contest concluded with 186 Iraqi tanks and 127 other armoured vehicles left in ruins. In exchange, four Abrams tanks were damaged and one of these was completely written off. Two Bradleys were lost, and debate continues as to whether the US losses were the result of enemy or friendly fire, or a combination of both. Two American

Soviet-built SA-13 antiaircraft missile systems, like this museum piece, were eliminated during the Battle of Medina Ridge. *(Creative Commons Vitaly V Kuzmin via Wikimedia Commons)*

A-10 Thunderbolt ground attack aircraft, such as these, took out numerous Iraqi tanks at Medina Ridge. *(US Air Force via Wikimedia Commons)*

With his men in the field, Colonel, later General Montgomery Meigs, commanded the 2nd Brigade, 1st Armored Division during the fight at Medina Ridge. *(US Army via Wikimedia Commons)*

An American M109 155mm self-propelled howitzer rolls forward towards action in the Gulf War. *(Creative Commons Fury 1991 via Wikimedia Commons)*

soldiers were killed in action and 33 wounded, while Iraqi casualties were estimated in the hundreds, with more than 800 taken prisoner.

More than three dozen Iraqi tanks were destroyed by Hellfire missiles and other ordnance delivered from AH-64 Apache attack helicopters and A-10 Thunderbolt ground support aircraft. Two Apaches and a single A-10 were shot down during the engagement. Prior to and during the Battle of Medina Ridge, the various air support units assigned to the 1st Armored Division flew continual sorties for 39 hours, maintaining air superiority and ranging ahead of the ground forces, while actively transporting troops to active areas, delivering supplies and ammunition, and evacuating wounded.

Iraqi field artillery opened fire on the advancing Americans near Medina Ridge to no appreciable result as its targets were beyond effective range, but in turn the Iraqis invited counterbattery fire from the US 75th Field Artillery Brigade, 2nd Battalion, 1st Field Artillery Regiment, and Battery B, 25th Field Artillery which silenced at least two enemy artillery battalions.

An American artillery battery maintains steady fire against Iraqi targets. *(Creative Commons Don Brunett via Wikimedia Commons)*

The 3rd Brigade, 3rd Infantry Division penetrated defences of the Iraqi Adnan Division and at least four other divisions sent to the support of the Medina Republican Guard. The Americans roughly handled every enemy formation encountered, eliminating 113 Iraqi tanks and armoured vehicles, 48 trucks, and three antiaircraft weapons along with bagging over 500 prisoners. One American soldier was killed in the brawl, and 33 were wounded as the two Bradleys were disabled in combat.

At the same time, the 3rd Brigade, 1st Armored Division destroyed an Iraqi armoured brigade and fought steadily for an entire 24-hour period. During that time, the American armoured brigade accounted for the elimination of 102 enemy tanks, 81 other armoured vehicles, 34 artillery pieces, and 15 anti-aircraft guns while capturing more than 500 enemy combatants. During its test of endurance, the 3rd Brigade, 1st Armored Division, lost no tanks or other vehicles and had only three men wounded.

The 2nd Brigade, 1st Armored Division, the heaviest American formation on the field, directly engaged the 2nd Brigade of the Medina Division and dispatched the enemy with alacrity. In less than an hour, the 2nd Brigade 'brewed up' 61 assorted Iraqi tanks, including T-55 and T-72 models, 34 other armoured vehicles, and five SA-13 surface-to-air missile batteries.

After decisively defeating the Iraqis at Medina Ridge, the 1st Armored Division and the 3rd Brigade, 3rd Infantry Division, continued their eastwards thrust towards the Kuwaiti border, as well as their mission to seek and destroy hostile tanks and troops prior to the announcement of the ceasefire on February 28. The Battle of Medina Ridge is cited as the largest engagement of the Gulf War by some sources, while others assert that the Battle of Objective Norfolk stakes that claim. In either case, the victories were instrumental in sounding the death knell of the Republican Guard.

Although defeated, the Iraqi formations of the Republican Guard Forces Command did earn the respect of their adversaries at Medina Ridge, unlike the thousands of inferior and virtually untrained soldiers and conscripts who had surrendered at the sight of Coalition forces in the early hours of the ground war. In the spring of 1991, Colonel Montgomery Meigs, commander of the 2nd Brigade, 1st Armored Division, and a descendant of a general of the American Civil War who bore the same name, was asked to assess the quality of the enemy his forces had faced in the battle at Medina Ridge. Meigs responded with praise: "These guys stayed and fought." ■

M 2/3 Bradley fighting vehicles, like this one silhouetted against the setting sun, performed admirably at Medina Ridge and elsewhere. *(US Air Force via Wikimedia Commons)*

BATTLE OF NORFOLK

JUST TWO HOURS after the conclusion of the action at 73 Easting, the VII Corps became involved in the largest tank battle of the Gulf War, and one of the largest tank versus tank engagements in the history of the US Army.

After completing its early mission at 73 Easting, the 2nd Armored Cavalry Regiment made way for VII Corps to pass through during its north-eastward turn, pressing on towards Objective Norfolk, an identified junction of the IPSA (Iraqi Pipeline to Saudi Arabia) road and numerous other arteries that constituted a vital Iraqi route, and depot for supply and reinforcement.

Conditions for battle were far from ideal as the engagement commenced shortly after midnight on February 27, 1991, in darkness and a soupy sludge of rain, fog, smoke soon to be punctuated by fires from burning vehicles. Veterans later described the hours of combat as "Fright Night".

From VII Corps, the 334 M1A1 Abrams tanks and 224 Bradley fighting vehicles of the US 2nd Armored and 1st Infantry Divisions, and other formations, constituted a formidable fighting force, while the British 1st Armoured Division, consisting of the 4th and 7th Armoured brigades with 157 Challenger 1 tanks, 135 Warrior infantry fighting vehicles, and 24 M-109 155mm self-propelled howitzers, was also arrayed for the coming fight. Task Force 1-41 (1st Battalion, 41st Infantry Regiment), 2nd Armored led the way forward, with the British 1st Armoured protecting the right flank of the advance. In the looming battle at Objective Norfolk, the combined Anglo-American firepower would annihilate the Iraqi Tawakalna Division of the Republican Guard, along with the enemy 18th Mechanized and 9th Armoured Brigades, and its 52nd Armoured Division.

By the time the Norfolk battle broke out, the VII Corps, under the command of General Frederick M Franks, had already been engaged in various locations during its advance from the Iraqi frontier. Task Force 1-41 had fought elements of the Republican Guard with the 3rd Battalion, 66th Armored Regiment – at the tip of the spear – taking out numerous Iraqi tanks and armoured fighting vehicles. In preliminary action, two Bradleys had been lost to enemy fire and three American soldiers killed during an ambush that soon resulted in the retaliatory destruction of an entire Iraqi battalion of T-55 tanks, and later fixed

This dug-in Iraqi T-72 tank was photographed during the heat of battle at Objective Norfolk. *(US Army via Wikimedia Commons)*

These entrenched Iraqi tanks were destroyed by Task Force 1-41 in the Battle of Norfolk. *(US Army via Wikimedia Commons)*

Soldiers of Task Force 1-41 pose with a destroyed Iraqi tank after the Battle of Norfolk. *(Creative Commons Fury 1991 via Wikimedia Commons)*

A gunner aboard an M1A1 of the 2nd Battalion, 34th Armored Regiment vividly described the heat of battle: "On February 27, we attacked elements of the Republican Guard at night," he recalled. "We had the advantage because our night sights are far superior to theirs. They didn't know we were there until we opened fire. And they couldn't fire back at us because, basically, they couldn't see us. We had two companies of scouts with us that came up on line and stopped. Then we just sat back and picked them off. Once the round hit, you could see the turrets just pop right off the enemy vehicles. They would burn for 35-40 minutes. The fuel and ammunition would keep it burning. And the rounds they stored in the tank would explode. They were trying to evade us, but the thermal sights we have, picked them up. We had orders to fire at will. It was a free-for-all."

When an Iraqi counterattack threatened the positions of the 4th Battalion, 3rd Field Artillery Regiment, a platoon of tanks from Task Force 1-41 eliminated every single enemy armoured vehicle.

positions along with an enemy team armed with rocket-propelled grenade (RPG) launchers. Along the IPSA road, 2nd Armoured units blasted 60 Iraqi tanks and 35 armoured fighting vehicles.

As the battle developed, the opposing forces became entangled amid the foul weather and fog of battle. The Coalition tankers and Bradley crews were able to utilise their superior target acquisition and ranging gear to great effect, engaging Iraqi armour at near standoff range before the enemy could fix and fire its own weapons. However, incidents of friendly fire were alarmingly high, and one of the worst episodes of the Gulf War occurred at Norfolk when US tanks mistakenly fired on their own troops, killing six and wounding 25, after mistaking the flashes of enemy hand grenades for opposing tank fire. Just a day earlier, another horrific incident had occurred when US A-10 Thunderbolt attack planes mistakenly targeted a column of Warrior vehicles and killed nine British soldiers, wounding 11.

At Objective Norfolk, the Iraqis bore the brunt of Coalition firepower and the effect was telling.

This T-55 tank of the Republican Guard was turned into twisted wreckage during the Battle of Norfolk. *(Creative Commons Don Brunett via Wikimedia Commons)*

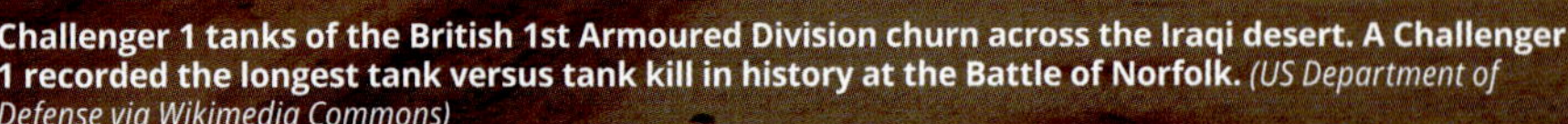

Challenger 1 tanks of the British 1st Armoured Division churn across the Iraqi desert. A Challenger 1 recorded the longest tank versus tank kill in history at the Battle of Norfolk. *(US Department of Defense via Wikimedia Commons)*

The reconnaissance team of Battery C, 4th Battalion, 3rd Field Artillery Regiment rolls past a burning Iraqi tank. *(Creative Commons Fury 1991 via Wikimedia Commons)*

The blackened hulk of an Iraqi T-55 tank lies derelict in the desert after a fight with Coalition armour. *(U.S. Army via Wikimedia Commons)*

The American unit went on to capture almost an entire Iraqi tank battalion on the day. The 1st Engineer Battalion added its considerable weight, destroying large caches of enemy ammunition and supplies, while taking out 58 Iraqi tanks and 41 anti-aircraft artillery weapons. Further action by the 2nd Battalion, 16th Infantry Regiment and 2nd Battalion, 34th Armored, eliminated the enemy 48th Infantry Division and the 9th Armoured Brigade, Tawakalna Division. The US 3rd Armored Division defeated two Iraqi divisions in simultaneous action at Objective Dorset, a component of the larger Norfolk engagement, eliminating 300 enemy armoured vehicles.

The British 1st Armoured Division, led by General Rupert Smith, had already accounted for more than 50 Iraqi tanks in a 90-minute battle between the 7th Brigade and the enemy 52nd Armored Division on February 26. Meanwhile, the 4th Brigade had eliminated enemy command-and-control facilities, along with artillery emplacements. The British armour and infantry engaged and defeated nearly four full Iraqi divisions, including the 25th, 26th, 31st, and 48th, before finishing off the 52nd Armoured Division in a series of sharp clashes.

In the Battle of Norfolk, a Challenger 1 tank of the Royal Scots Dragoon Guards 'brewed up' an Iraqi tank at a range of more than three miles, the longest tank versus tank battlefield kill in modern warfare. Both the 4th and 7th Brigades

wreaked havoc among the enemy formations and fortifications, while two Warriors were lost to friendly fire in the chaotic affair. British forces dominated their encounters with the Iraqi armed forces, reaching several interim objectives – nicknamed Steel, Copper, Zinc, Brass, and Bronze – with dash while eliminating another 145 enemy tanks and armoured personnel vehicles, and rounding up 1,850 prisoners. At objective Platinum, elements of the 1st Armoured Division completely erased an Iraqi tank company.

All the while, Coalition artillery and air support were timely and accurate. Iraqi artillery did not factor in the fighting as at least 70 guns were silenced at objective Tungsten alone.

During the single day of armoured confrontation at Objective Norfolk and environs, the fate of Iraqi arms was sealed. The awesome, deadly VII Corps had demonstrated clear superiority in the decimation of opposing armour, destroying well over 1,600 tanks and armoured vehicles and taking more than 21,000 prisoners, while inflicting an unknown but heavy number of killed and wounded on the enemy. The vaunted Tawakalna Division ceased to exist as a viable fighting force.

The Coalition forces sustained 36 killed in action and 110 wounded. Five M1A1 tanks were destroyed, each of them attributed directly to friendly fire and struck by lethal depleted uranium rounds. Five Bradleys were lost along with the two Warriors, and three Challengers were damaged.

The Coalition victory at Objective Norfolk was complete and overwhelming. After the fighting ended at Objective Dorset on February 28, a cease fire was declared the same day. ■

Iraqi tanks destroyed by Task Force 1-41 litter the desert during the Gulf War. *(Creative Commons Fury 1991 via Wikimedia Commons)*

Crewmen of the Royal Scots Dragoon Guards pause with their Challenger 1 tank during Operation Desert Storm. *(US Army via Wikimedia Commons)*

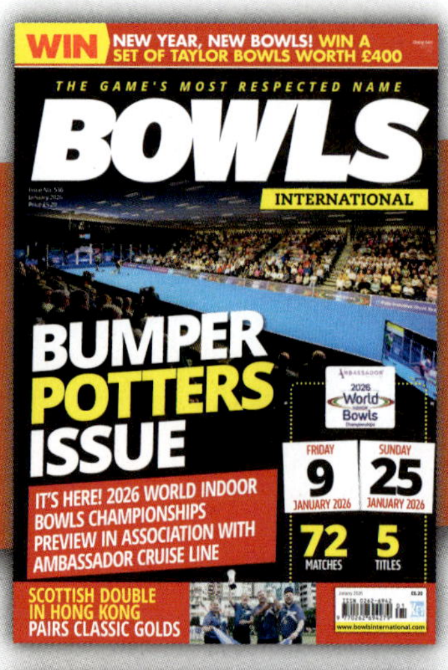

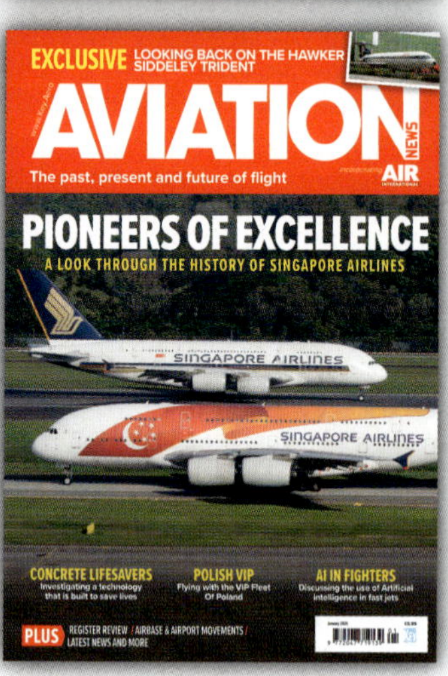

Enjoy one of our many titles today!

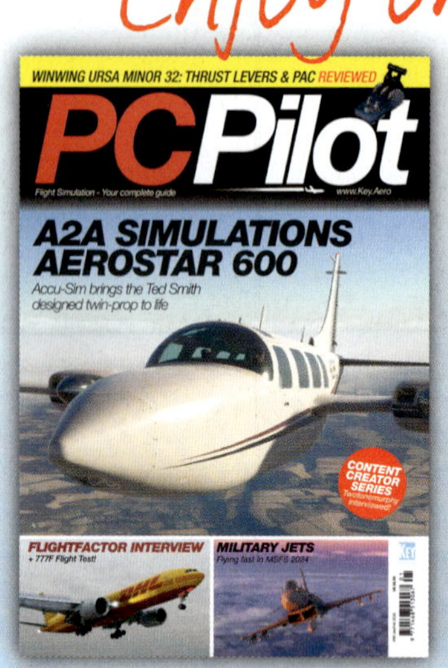

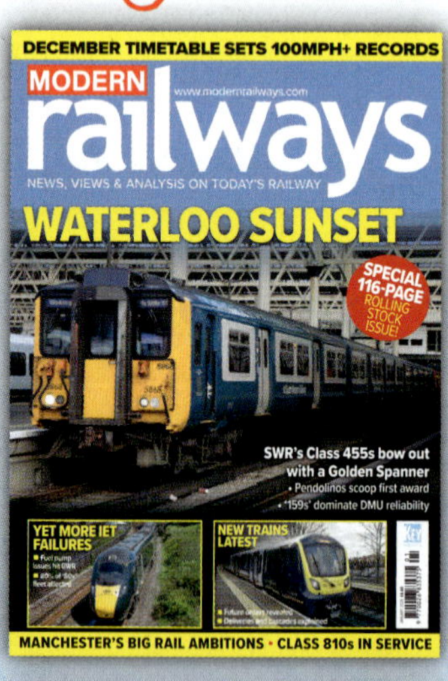

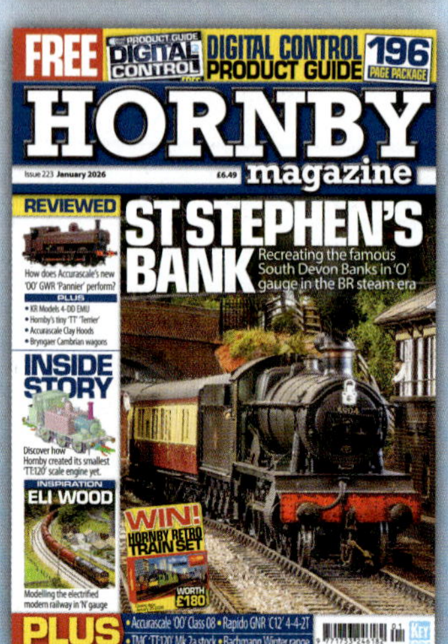

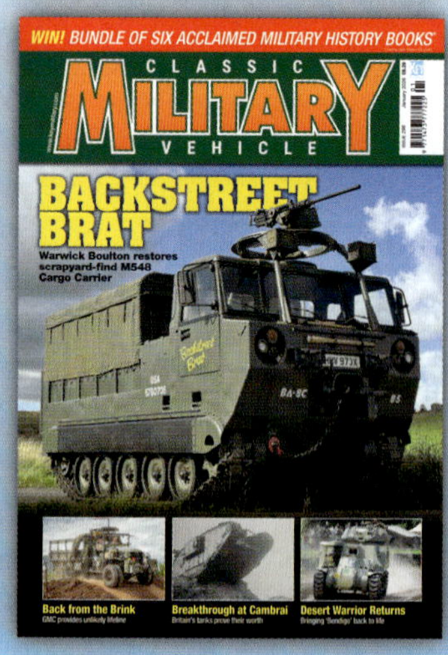

SUBSCRIBE TODAY!

Our historic and informative magazines cover a wide array of topics from around the world. From Aviation and Aircraft to Modelling, Public Transport and Railways to Classic Vehicles, Military History and more, we're sure you'll find something you can't put down.

With Digital and Print magazine subscriptions allowing you to find out more about your favourite topic in the format that is most comfortable for you, why not treat yourself to a subscription that'll take your interest to the next level today?

SOME REASONS TO SUBSCRIBE TO ONE OF OUR FANTASTIC MAGAZINES

» **EXCLUSIVE** Subscriber offers on the *Key Publishing* Shop » **SAVE** over buying individual issues
» **DELIVERED DIRECT** to your door » **BE THE FIRST** to read the latest features
» **SUBSCRIBER DISCOUNTS** on *Key Publishing* event tickets

Scan the QR code TODAY to order direct from our shop!

shop.keypublishing.com/collections/all-subscriptions
or call **+44 (0)1780 480404** (Lines open 9.00-5.30, Monday-Friday GMT)

KUWAIT INTERNATIONAL AIRPORT

THEY HAD SWIFTLY breached the defences of Saddam Hussein's forces on the Kuwaiti frontier and slashed their way across the desert. In the process, the US 1st and 2nd Marine Divisions, and the 2nd Armored Division's Tiger Brigade of the US Army, had left hundreds of enemy tanks burning hulks and scooped up thousands of prisoners, many of them eager to surrender to the Coalition juggernaut.

One of the last, but also one of the most significant objectives of the direct thrust into Kuwait, was the capture of the international airport in the southern sector of Kuwait City. Along the way, the Marines and Army formations had taken on elements of no fewer than 18 divisions of the Iraqi armed forces. The defenders were never able to stem the tide, and in three days of fighting, the Iraqis were routed and the airport was in American hands.

Co-ordinating with US Special Forces inserted to help clear the airport buildings of enemy snipers and pockets of diehard resistance, the Marine divisions began the final operations to secure the airport on February 27, 1991. The 1st and 2nd Marine Divisions approached their objectives inside the capital city from different directions.

When the 1st Marine Division reached the edge of the international airport, they encountered defenders from the Iraqi 12th Armoured Brigade, 3rd Armoured Division, along with the remnants of other armoured formations, including a few T-62 tanks and infantry units, scattered in the vicinity. The exposed Iraqi tanks were taken under fire at a safe distance,

most of them going up in flames as they were hit by TOW anti-tank missiles. Within a few hours, the Iraqi 3rd Armoured Division had effectively ceased to exist, its cumulative losses in three days of fighting reaching 320 T-55, T-62, and T-72 Soviet-made tanks.

The 2nd Marine Division and the Tiger Brigade, with its 3rd Battalion, 41st Infantry Regiment 'Straight and Stalwart Battalion Task

General Ra'ad al-Hamdani commented on Iraqi tactics in the aftermath of the fight for Kuwait International Airport. *(US Government via Wikimedia Commons)*

Marine artillerymen prepare to open fire on Iraqi positions during the drive into Kuwait. *(US Marine Corps via Wikimedia Commons)*

Force' leading the advance, fought their way towards the complex of hangars and buildings at Kuwait International Airport. By nightfall on February 26, the entire airport perimeter was surrounded. While enemy activity was ongoing inside the airport warren of buildings and hangars, large numbers of other Iraqis, along with their tanks and armoured vehicles, were attempting to flee north from Kuwait City towards the Iraqi frontier. These columns were in the open and assailed not only by Coalition ground forces, but also from the air.

Coalition naval and air forces bombarded enclaves of enemy troops holed up on the grounds of Kuwait International Airport. Reports indicated that the battleships USS *Wisconsin* and USS *Missouri* employed their heavy 16in main batteries to soften up the enemy positions. The airport was soon wreathed in smoke, and fires had broken out among the buildings hit by naval gunfire. The Marines and Army troops moved in and began clearing the airport, wary of enemy sniper fire

This British Airways Boeing 747 passenger jet was blown up after Iraqi forces seized Kuwait International Airport in August 1990. *(US Department of Defense via Wikimedia Commons)*

Members of the 1st Marine Division pause after the fighting at Kuwait International Airport has ended. *(US Department of Defense via Wikimedia Commons)*

Destroyed aircraft litter the tarmac of Kuwait International Airport during the Gulf War. *(US Navy via Wikimedia Commons)*

and possible booby traps. Special forces troops advanced quickly from structure to structure to root out Iraqi soldiers that still resisted.

Even as Kuwait International Airport was being secured, tactical air traffic control became a priority. Air Force personnel moved in to establish temporary communications, bringing equipment with them, and also attempting to repair infrastructure that had been damaged during the Iraqi occupation and the fight for control of the facilities. Marine Air Traffic Squadron 38 arrived to establish approach air traffic control in supervision of upcoming arrivals and departures.

During the three days of fighting to reach Kuwait International Airport, the Marines engaged in the largest collective tank battle, or series of battles, in their storied history. The victory was significant, not only in the establishment of supply and logistics links, but also in symbolic recognition of the impending Coalition victory in Operation Desert Storm. The liberation of the airport sparked spontaneous celebrations in Kuwait City as civilians responded to the departure of their Iraqi oppressors.

Control of Kuwait International Airport was one of the last actions in the ground war of Desert Storm, signalling the final hours of hostilities. In retrospect, Republican Guard General Ra'ad al-Hamdani attributed the defeat of Iraqi forces at the airport largely to flawed tactics. In a postwar interview, he commented: "We had a problem of inflexibility of usage with the armoured forces. We always favoured tying the infantry to tank divisions."

While there is no doubt that the general's assessment is accurate, there was obviously more to the story. Coalition forces had prevailed in large measure due to a substantial technology advantage over outmoded Soviet-era equipment, as well as the flexibility and initiative of officers and soldiers in the field, overwhelmingly superior firepower on land, at sea, and in the air, and the sheer speed and audacity with which the liberating forces advanced. ■

US Marines and their light armoured vehicles roll into Kuwait International Airport after securing the area. *(US Department of Defense via Wikimedia Commons)*

Destroyed and abandoned vehicles, civilian and military, are strewn along Highway 80, the so-called Highway of Death. *(US Air Force via Wikimedia Commons)*

ALONG THE HIGHWAY OF DEATH

FOR RETREATING IRAQI soldiers, the death dealing drama that unfolded on an open highway between Kuwait City and the supposed sanctuary of Basra in their home country could scarcely have been imagined – either by the attackers or those on the receiving end of a terrible bludgeoning from air and land.

Aware that their occupation of Kuwait was being forcibly brought to a close, thousands of Iraqi soldiers decided their best course of action was to leave the Kuwaiti capital and strike out along the highway towards their homeland. Their occupation of Kuwait had been brutal, but the overwhelming might of the Coalition forces unleashed in Desert Storm had made the outcome of the brief Persian Gulf War inevitable and set the stage for incredible retribution.

Years after the Gulf War, the rusting hulk of an Iraqi tank and the sole of an old shoe remain as mute testament to the fury of the Highway of Death. *(Creative Commons Christiaan Briggs via Wikimedia Commons)*

Probably unaware of the horror that would befall them, retreating Iraqi troops and some civilians sympathetic to Saddam Hussein (possibly Palestinians living in the country), and others, took to their tanks, armoured vehicles, and civilian cars and trucks on February 26-27, at the height of the 100-hour ground

Burned out Iraqi military vehicles are strung out along the Highway of Death. *(US Department of Defense via Wikimedia Commons)*

The highway between Kuwait City and Basra is choked with vehicles abandoned by fleeing Iraqi soldiers. *(US Navy via Wikimedia Commons)*

This Iraqi tank lies a mass of twisted steel after being struck by a Coalition missile. *(US Air Force via Wikimedia Commons)*

war. They set out travelling north on six-lane Highway 80, the broad thoroughfare that led to Basra through the border town of Safwan.

Soon enough, however, a lengthy column of vehicles was discovered and set upon by Coalition aircraft. For ten hours, Highway 80 became the scene of a devastating attack. Coalition ground forces also contributed to the utter decimation of the enemy forces attempting to flee, although some sources have estimated that a large number of Iraqi soldiers, perhaps as many as 80,000, made good their escape. Still, there was ample evidence of a slaughter on an immense scale. The number of Iraqis killed in the action along what became known as the Highway of Death is unknown, but estimates range upwards of 1,000.

The Coalition onslaught supposedly began when Grumman A-6 Intruder attack aircraft pressed home attacks against the head and rear of a column strung out for some distance on the open road. The Intruders of the 3rd Marine Aircraft Wing struck with Mk 20 Rockeye II cluster bombs, disabling vehicles at both ends and trapping those in between. From there, the attacks escalated steadily as naval aircraft from the carrier USS *Ranger* and USAF planes joined in the assault. Vehicles that were boxed in were blasted by missiles, bombs, and cannon shells. Occupants abandoned them, taking to their heels. US A-10 attack planes flew low and slow over the unfolding devastation, loosing bombs and shooting up targets with rounds from their 30mm nose cannon. One pilot related: "It was like shooting fish in a barrel."

One reporter wrote: "This six-lane highway had brought most of the Iraqi troops into Kuwait. Now they were trying desperately trying to get out, and they chose the same route from which they had entered. Coalition intelligence picked up the traffic immediately. In came the air strikes led by the A-10 Warthog. Other aircraft followed; F-16s, F-15s. Anything that had a bomb on it. I spoke with a pilot involved in the operation. He told me it was like being in a shooting gallery... scorched vehicles lined the highway."

The few vehicles that were extricated from the massive traffic jam and resulting kill zone were later attacked by ground forces, including the Tiger Brigade of the US Army's 2nd Armored Division, which occupied high ground north of Kuwait City near a narrowing in the route. Tiger Brigade possessed an excellent field of fire in all directions from its positions along Mutla Ridge, and a section of the roadway near a local police station nicknamed Mile of Death.

General Norman Schwarzkopf, commanding Coalition forces, had ordered the destruction of the Iraqi ability to wage aggressive war and explained the devastating onslaught in a postwar interview. "The first reason why we bombed the highway coming out of Kuwait is because there was a great deal of military equipment on that highway," he explained, "and I had given orders to all my commanders that I wanted every piece of Iraqi equipment that we possibly could destroy. Secondly, this was not a bunch of innocent people just trying to make their way back across the border to Iraq. This was a bunch of rapists, murderers and thugs who had raped and pillaged downtown Kuwait City and now were trying to get out of the country before they were caught."

Two M1A1 Abrams tanks flank a knocked out Iraqi T-55 tank on the Highway of Death. *(US Marine Corps via Wikimedia Commons)*

had engaged the retreating Republican Guard along Highway 8 and destroyed 400 trucks, along with 185 armoured vehicles. The number of enemy soldiers killed probably topped 300.

One Iraqi survivor of the ordeal told the *Washington Post* newspaper in a 1993 interview: "There were hundreds of cars destroyed, soldiers screaming… It was night time as the bombs fell, lighting up charred cars, bodies on the side of the road and soldiers sprawled on the ground, hit by cluster bombs as they tried to escape from their vehicles. I saw hundreds of soldiers like this, but my main objective was to reach Basra. We arrived on foot."

Journalists who followed Coalition forces on the ground attempted to describe what they had seen, some of them trying to take a tally of the bodies lying around them. British journalist Robert Fisk, often critical of US foreign policy in the Middle East, reported that he had "lost count of the Iraqi corpses crammed into the smouldering wreckage or slumped face down in the sand." Others witnessed a veritable line of dead soldiers stretching for miles along the road.

Within a few hours, images of incredible destruction had filtered into the halls of the US

The rusting barrel of a knocked out Iraqi tank protrudes from its empty turret in the desert. *(Creative Commons Christiaan Briggs via Wikimedia Commons)*

A Coalition soldier examines the hulk of a destroyed Iraqi tank that has been painted with graffiti by others on the Highway of Death. *(US Air Force via Wikimedia Commons)*

A USAF officer echoed the general's observation. "I think we're past the point of just letting Saddam Hussein get in his tanks and drive them back into Iraq and say 'I'm sorry'. I feel fairly punitive about it."

Although US Navy Commander Frank Sweigert told a newspaper reporter that the Iraqis were "like sitting ducks," he added, "one side of me says 'That's right, it's like shooting ducks in a pond. Does that make me uncomfortable? Not necessarily. Except there is a side of me that says, 'What are they dying for? For a madman's cause? And is that fair?' Well, we're at war; it's the tragedy of war, but we do our jobs."

Further along the route of escape, it has been confirmed that Iraqi combat troops of the elite Republican Guard Hammurabi Division were attempting to reach safety along a spur of Highway 80 that was designated Highway 8. A battalion of AH-64 Apache attack helicopters swooped in and smashed scores of vehicles, while US Army artillery units opened fire, and blackened hulks were strewn across a 50-mile stretch of roadway and the surrounding desert. By the afternoon and evening of February 27, the Army's 24th Infantry Division (Mechanized)

This Iraqi self-propelled howitzer lies a blackened shell after a direct hit on the Highway of Death. *(US Navy via Wikimedia Commons)*

US Navy Grumman A-6 Intruder attack aircraft, like this one laden with bombs, sowed destruction on Highway 80 out of Kuwait City. *(US Navy via Wikimedia Commons)*

government, and numerous sources aver that these had a telling influence on the decision of President George HW Bush to order a ceasefire. For the Coalition, victory in battle was one thing, while simple slaughter was quite another. Bush contacted Schwarzkopf and asked that arrangements be made to stop the killing.

One image captured by photojournalist Ken Jarecke was so grisly that it was withheld by many news outlets that chose to avoid criticism for mass publication. The photo shows an Iraqi soldier burned beyond recognition as he is caught in death while attempting to climb out of the front window of a truck that has been set ablaze. "There was supposed to be a ceasefire in about an hour, maybe an hour and a half," remembered Jarecke. "We had travelled east from Nasiriya towards Basra, hooked up with Highway 80 and we started south towards Kuwait City. And we came across this… just a single lorry, kind of in the middle of a double

An armoured personnel carrier of the 7th Brigade Royal Scots advances through debris of war on the Highway of Death. *(US Navy via Wikimedia Commons)*

lane highway… I said, 'If I don't make pictures like this, people like my mother will think what they see in war is what they see in the movies'."

Chairman of the Joint Chiefs of Staff General Colin Powell recalled the situation in an interview for the US Public Broadcasting System series *Frontline*. "We were also starting to see some scenes that were unpleasant. The 'Highway of Death'… it may be a horrible name to give it and sort of gives it an emotional contact, but that's what the press were calling it. At the so-called highway of death where people were being slaughtered as our planes went up and down.

"You don't do unnecessary killing if it can be avoided," Powell continued. "At some point you decide you have accomplished your objectives and you stop. And on that morning both General Schwarzkopf and I thought that we were on the verge of accomplishing our objectives and we were in the window of putting an end to it, so there was not unnecessary additional loss of life on the part of American and Coalition forces, or on the part of Iraqi youngsters…"

Despite the decision to halt offensive operations, controversy did surface. Some critics cited United Nations Resolution 660 passed in August 1990 that had demanded the withdrawal of Iraqi forces from Kuwait, stating that the soldiers who were attacked were actually trying to comply with the resolution.

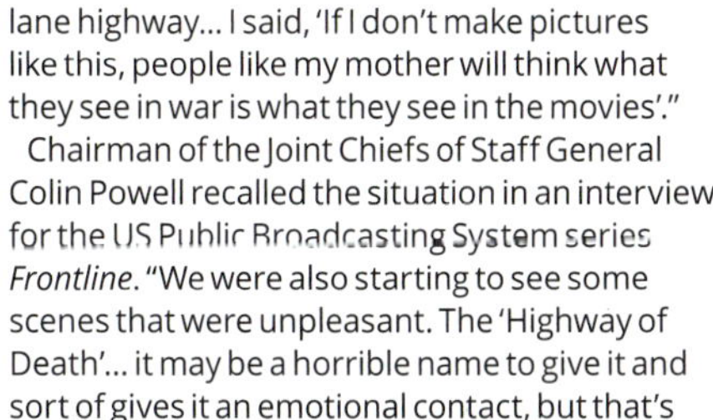

Abandoned cars and trucks along the highway out of Kuwait City, left by retreating Iraqi soldiers. *(US Navy via Wikimedia Commons)*

Abandoned Mitsubishi and Mercedes trucks flank a destroyed tank on the Highway of Death.
(US Marine Corps via Wikimedia Commons)

However, most observers believed this was a stretch. The soldiers were retreating, but they retained their tanks and other weapons.

Former US Attorney General Ramsey Clark was vocal in condemning the offensive action. Clark called the one-sided assault a violation of the Geneva Convention's Article 3, which said that soldiers not engaged in combat due to illness, wounds, or prisoner status could not be killed. Still, the fact remained that the Iraqis were armed and attempting to escape Coalition forces.

Allegations of war crimes were levied against Coalition leaders, including President Bush,

This transport truck with a flatbed trailer and armoured personnel carrier lie riddled with shrapnel on the road out of Kuwait City.
(US Navy via Wikimedia Commons)

Vice President Dan Quayle, Generals Powell and Schwarzkopf, and others, but never gained widespread support, even though inflammatory rhetoric was filed by Clark and his cohorts with the International War Crimes Tribunal in 1992. Clark claimed that US military personnel pursued their attacks with callous disregard. "More than 750 vehicles were destroyed," the report said of the Highway of Death engagement. "Thousands were killed without US casualties. A US commander said: "We really waxed them." It was called a Turkey Shoot. One Apache helicopter crew member yelled: "Say hello to Allah" as he launched a laser-guided Hellfire missile.

Some time after hostilities ceased, *Time* magazine published an extensive story on the Highway of Death, reporting: "The pictures were among the most stunning to come out of the Gulf War; mile after mile of burned, smashed, shattered vehicles of every description – tanks, armored cars, trucks, autos, even stolen Kuwaiti fire trucks – littering the highway from Kuwait City to Basra. To some Americans, the pictures were also sickening. After the war, correspondents did find some cars and trucks with burned bodies, but also many vehicles that had been abandoned. Their occupants had fled on foot, and the American planes often did not fire at them."

For some, the postwar discourse may have obscured the plain truth that Iraqi aggression against Kuwait, the brutality of their occupation, the pillaging of their neighbouring country, had caused the Gulf War in the first place. Further, the harsh fact remained that war means death and destruction – and it cannot be refined. ■

AH-64 Apache attack helicopters like this example destroyed targets along the Highway of Death.
(US Army via Wikimedia Commons)

BEHIND THE LINES – SPECIAL OPERATIONS

General Norman Schwarzkopf addresses members of Delta Force in the Persian Gulf region.
(US Department of Defense via Wikimedia Commons)

COVERT OPERATIONS, INHERENTLY risky and problematic in planning and execution, did contribute significantly to Coalition military operations before and during Desert Storm.

Among the first Coalition forces to go into harm's way were those of Task Force Normandy, assigned to take out Iraqi radar and early warning systems in advance of the air offensive that began on January 17, 1991. One officer described the effort as "… one of the smallest yet most successful and important joint Army-Air Force operations in the initial strikes in Operation Desert Storm…"

At least two specific Iraqi sites were located, and their elimination would open a 20-mile-wide corridor for strike aircraft to attack targets deep inside Iraq, the possibility of detection and interdiction by enemy aircraft, missiles, or anti-aircraft fire greatly diminished should Task Force Normandy succeed in the mission. Carrying out the covert strike were nine AH-64 Apache helicopters of the US Army's 1st Battalion, 101st Aviation Regiment, 101st Airborne Division (Air Assault) supported by four MH-53J Pave Low helicopters of the US Air Force 20th Special Operations Squadron that provided navigational assistance and electronic countermeasures to thwart detection. MH-47E Chinook helicopters of the Army's 160th Special Operations Aviation Regiment (SOAR) 'Night Stalkers' refuelled the Apaches in the air.

Flying from a temporary staging base at Al Jouf, Saudi Arabia, the task force entered Iraqi air space just after 2am, and separate teams attacked eastern and western targets. Altering course in a zigzag pattern, the Americans avoided desert nomad camps and utilised terrain features such as dunes and wadis for cover, maintaining altitude of no more than 50ft above the desert floor. The Pave Low crews were challenged by desert winds and heat that affected visibility, increasing their reliance on onboard sensors and computer equipment. At the appropriate time, the Pave Lows dropped glowing sticks to the ground to mark locations for the incoming Apaches.

Immediately, an Iraqi sentry looked up to the sky and began sprinting for a ground control bunker. Just as he reached the door, an Apache's laser guided AGM-114 Hellfire missile crashed into the structure. Simultaneously, the command centre was struck by Hydra 70 rockets. In seconds, the building and a pair of communications vans were destroyed. The other identified radar site was eliminated just five seconds later, erupting in a huge ball of fire. The entire offensive action was concluded in only four minutes.

One Pave Low co-pilot remembered shouting: "They did it! They did it! I felt like I was on the 50-yard line of a football game yelling, 'Go! Go! Go!'"

The drama of the Task Force Normandy mission, however, was not quite finished. As the helicopters retired, one Pave Low was locked onto by a pair Iraqi SA-7 surface-to-air missiles after crossing back into Saudi air space. Crewmen observing the missiles thought they were on target and shouted

Delta Force bodyguards surround General Norman Schwarzkopf during Desert Storm.
(US Department of Defense via Wikimedia Commons)

Members of Delta Force engage in Scud hunting behind Iraqi lines. *(US Special Operations Command via Wikimedia Commons)*

Through the course of the Gulf War, special operations forces of the United States and Great Britain were engaged in varied operations inside enemy territory. These included hunting of fixed and mobile Iraqi Scud missile launchers, either to destroy them immediately or pinpoint their locations for destruction by air assets. The elimination of the Scud threat was a priority from the outset, particularly as they targeted civilian population centres in Saudi Arabia and Israel. Other missions involved reconnaissance and intelligence gathering, as special operations troops established hidden observation posts and transmitted information on Iraqi troop movements in real time and marked high value targets for air strikes. In addition, special forces conducted diversionary raids to draw Iraqi attention away from primary areas of Coalition operations, disabled enemy communications centres and infrastructure, and conducted combat search and rescue operations.

Coalition special operations units involved in Desert Storm crossed service branches and became models of teamwork. Along with the British SAS and SBS, the US Army Special Forces, or Green Berets, worked in tandem with Delta Force as the 5th and 10th Special Forces Groups contributed troops. The USAF Special Operations Command brought aviation support, its units also joining with Delta Force in Scud-hunting activities. US Navy SEALs (Sea, Air, and Land) seized Iraqi offshore oil platforms that had been converted to anti-aircraft weapons sites and carried out Visit, Board, Search, and Seizure to enforce blockade restrictions during Desert Shield. The SEALs also participated in the highly successful strategic ruse that diverted Iraqi troops from the main line of advance when the ground phase of Desert Storm commenced. Along with the US and British special operations commitment, Syrian and Saudi special forces were deployed co-operatively.

In the aftermath of the Gulf War, the story of Bravo Two Zero, an intrepid eight-man team from B Squadron 22 SAS emerged to illustrate the extreme hazards of special operations and became a subject of lingering controversy regarding the actual circumstances of the ill-fated mission it undertook.

This escape map was used by a member of SAS team Bravo Two Zero. *(Creative Commons JebelAntar via Wikimedia Commons)*

Soldiers of the US Army 10th Special Forces Group return from the Persian Gulf, March 1991. *(US Department of Defense via Wikimedia Commons)*

One of three SAS teams with similar missions, Bravo Two Zero was inserted into the trackless Iraqi desert on the night of January 22-23 to locate and eliminate Iraqi Scud launchers. After insertion by RAF Chinook helicopter, the situation rapidly deteriorated for the team, led by Sergeant Steven Billy Mitchell, who later wrote an account of the mission under the pen name Andy McNab. Communications could not be established, and the presence of the team was discovered, leaving only the option to exfiltrate from enemy territory.

Two hundred miles inside Iraq, Bravo Two Zero encountered numbing cold during its

for evasive action. The pilot broke away and jettisoned flares to draw the missiles away. Infrared countermeasures and a violent manoeuvre averted disaster. The mission was accomplished without loss.

Later, on the first night of the air campaign, a Chinook of the 160th SOAR was observed by Iraqi soldiers disguised as desert nomads. As the helicopter flew its assigned route, an SA-7 was fired, causing the pilot to make a rapid descent. The hard landing that resulted damaged the helicopter's landing gear. The crew coaxed the CH-47 back into the air, reaching base safely, and making final descent onto mattresses laid out to soften the impact.

Some reports have suggested that General Norman Schwarzkopf, commander of Coalition forces during Desert Storm, was reluctant to deploy special operations forces, although he did utilise some members of the US Army's elite Delta Force as his personal bodyguard. However, British General Sir Peter de la Billière, serving as Schwarzkopf's deputy, harboured no such reservations. He had served with the Special Air Service (SAS) and counted on its covert combat prowess, along with that of the Special Boat Service (SBS).

An RAF CH-47 Chinook helicopter flies over the desert landscape. *(Government of the United Kingdom via Wikimedia Commons)*

first night. "We found a perfect lying-up place," wrote Mitchell as McNab in his 1993 bestseller titled *Bravo Two Zero*, "dead ground, out of sight and with cover from enemy fire… It was time to transmit our first Sit Rep [situation report] back to SAS camp in Saudi, telling them where we were and what state we were in…We waited for the acknowledgment but none came. If the SAS base didn't hear you, the rule was that you trekked back to the landing site and rendezvoused at a set time with a helicopter to pick up new radios."

The team members were unaware that their messages were being received but that they could not receive any return communications.

Complicating the situation, a shepherd boy stumbled upon the Bravo Two Zero camp the next morning, compromising its cover. Moving south towards the expected helicopter rendezvous point, the SAS men, according to Mitchell, engaged in a fierce firefight with a large number of Iraqi soldiers, inflicting many casualties and emerging unscathed themselves. Attempts to contact an AWACS airborne surveillance crew failed,

US Navy SEALs train with gas masks in place during the Gulf War. *(US Government via Wikimedia Commons)*

The MH-60 Blackhawk helicopter was regularly used during Gulf War special operations. *(US Army via Wikimedia Commons)*

and Mitchell decided to move north towards the Syrian border. During the hours that followed, the eight men became separated. Three continued toward Syria, and one died of hypothermia. Another perished later in the terrible cold. A third was killed during a clash with Iraqi civilians and local police. Three, including Mitchell, were taken prisoner.

Those captured by the Iraqis were moved multiple times during six weeks of captivity, and for a while they were held in the infamous Abu Ghraib prison, 20 miles west of Baghdad. Mitchell provided a harrowing account of their treatment, including excruciating torture and mental anguish. "As the kicks connected with my skull," he wrote of one beating, "there was a hissing, popping sound in my ears, and as I clenched my jaw, I heard the bones creak together. I felt blood trickle out of my ears and down my face… At one point we were driven out onto the streets

US Navy SEALs train with Desert Patrol Vehicles (DPV), popularly known as dune buggies. *(US Navy via Wikimedia Commons)*

and exhibited to roaring crowds of people – women with sticks, men with guns or stones, all waving pictures of Saddam Hussein."

While the captive trio endured, the eighth member of Bravo Two Zero, Corporal Colin Armstrong, who later wrote an account of the ordeal under the pen name Chris Ryan, experienced an incredible story of survival. Eluding capture, he walked approximately 180 miles to the Syrian frontier in the longest such journey of an SAS trooper or possibly any other soldier in history.

Although Armstrong's story and that of Mitchell both remain the subject of scrutiny and conjecture, Armstrong related a compelling account of his week-long trek. As he crossed the desert, he suffered from bone-chilling cold, drank water tainted with toxic material released by a nearby Iraqi nuclear facility, and nearly went mad.

In February 2021, Armstrong told *Force News*: "So for the last three nights I had nothing and I was walking about 40 kilometres (25 miles) a night. I started hallucinating and seeing visions of my daughter. It was that vivid I was putting my hand out to get a hold of her and she was talking to me." When he finally reached the town of Abu Kamal, Syria, he had lost a reported 38lb in weight.

Armstrong related that the Syrians treated him well, even giving him a new set of clothes before handing him over to officials at the British embassy in Damascus. The three prisoners were released in March 1991 – and mystery still shrouds the ordeal of Bravo Two Zero.

Special operations contributions to the Coalition war effort were substantial, though fraught with danger. On January 21, a US Navy F-14 fighter was shot down, and Air Force special operations Pararescue personnel flew in aboard an MH-53 helicopter to rescue the downed pilot. However, the radar intercept officer was taken prisoner. During the battle for the Saudi border town of Khafji, an AC-130 Spectre gunship of Air Force Special

Four MH-53 Pave Low helicopters fly over the open sea during training exercises.
(US Air Force via Wikimedia Commons)

Operations Command was shot down by an enemy missile, killing all 14 aboard in the largest loss of life in the command's history.

On the night before the ground offensive began, special operations teams numbering as few as three and as many as eight or more, were inserted at least 150 miles into Iraq to support the advances of the XVIII Airborne Corps and VII Corps. They relayed information on Scud missile deployments

The MH-53 Pave Low helicopter was instrumental in special operations during Desert Storm.
(US Government via Wikimedia Commons)

US Air Force Pararescue personnel participate in an exercise. Pararescue operations saved downed airmen in the Gulf War.
(US Air Force via Wikimedia Commons)

Iraqi Scud missiles such as these were hunted by Coalition special forces. *(US Department of Defense via Wikimedia Commons)*

Shoulder-fired SA-7 missiles such as this example targeted Task Force Normandy. *(Creative Commons DVIDSHUB via Wikimedia Commons)*

and watched for movement by elite Iraqi Republican Guard elements. Most of these teams were flown in by helicopter at night, individual soldiers carrying provisions, communications equipment, weapons

and ammunition that often weighed more than 100lb. They were usually required to walk some distance from their insertion point to establish hiding positions and camouflage the locations before daybreak.

One such team, the eight men of Special Forces Operational Detachment Alpha 525 (SFODA 525) of the 5th Special Forces Group, was inserted by two MH-60 helicopters on February 23, 1991, and assigned to take up observation positions along Highway 7, an important roadway running from Baghdad through the valley of the Euphrates River. After digging in just over 300yds from the highway prior to sunrise, the team remained secluded for some time.

However, as daylight came, a number of Iraqi civilians were observed in the area, which was more heavily populated than intelligence reports had indicated. Inevitably, the hiding place was discovered by three small children. Rather than harm the children, the team allowed them to leave the immediate vicinity. Soon afterwards, an adult male with more children approached the location. He was allowed to run away at the sight of the Americans, but the situation rapidly escalated. SFODA 525 was soon confronted by a force of approximately 150 Iraqi soldiers.

Accounts of the day-long action relate that 40 Iraqis were killed and many others wounded

A Chinook helicopter of the 5th Special Forces Group operates in the Middle East. *(US Government via Wikimedia Commons)*

in the first ten minutes of the ensuing fight. Threatened several times with being overrun, the team called for air support. Bombs were dropped dangerously close to their positions, but the timely air intervention helped turn the tide. Communicating with the aircraft by radio and signal mirrors, SFODA 525 held its ground, and by late afternoon an estimated 300 enemy troops had been killed.

As the sun set, SFODA 525 withdrew to a designated exfiltration area where two MH-60 helicopters airlifted them to safety at King Fahd International Airport in Dammam, Saudi Arabia. Miraculously, none of the Army Green Berets were killed or wounded.

British and American special operations worked together in a memorable mission to disrupt Iraqi communications. Infiltrating the suburbs of Baghdad via Chinook helicopters, a combined force of SBS and American members of the Army's Intelligence Support Activity unit scoured an area for underground fibre optic cable that the

The MH-60 variant of the Blackhawk helicopter is used by the 160th SOAR. *(US Army via Wikimedia Commons)*

Iraqis used to network with mobile Scud launchers. After two hours of digging, the cables were located and blown up.

One of the most memorable exploits of the Gulf War again involved the SBS and a swift operation into Kuwait City on February 28. The SBS assault team fast-roped from hovering CH-47 and Sea King helicopters into the US Embassy compound, rapidly securing the space. Prime Minister John Major reported triumphantly: "They are cleaning up, and I hope very much that the British ambassador will be able to return very speedily, perhaps as early as tomorrow."

Elsewhere on the final day of the ground war, Delta Force sniper teams located and destroyed 26 Scud missiles, preventing a last death-dealing gasp from Saddam Hussein's defeated arsenal and providing an emphatic coda to the contribution of special operations in the Gulf War. ■

Westland Sea King helicopters similar to this example participated in the SBS operation to take the British embassy in Kuwait City. *(US Government via Wikimedia Commons)*

An AH-64 Apache attack helicopter comes in for a landing. Apaches of the 101st were involved in Task Force Normandy. *(US Government via Wikimedia Commons)*

Retreating Iraqi soldiers set fire to Kuwaiti oil wells, creating an economic and environmental disaster. *(US Army Corps of Engineers via Wikimedia Commons)*

DECISION TO CEASEFIRE

THE FIGHT WAS a one-sided affair, and on February 28, 1991, President George HW Bush, after consulting with partner Coalition leaders, announced the suspension of offensive military operations in Desert Storm. On the face of it, the decision was simple – Iraq's military had been utterly defeated on the battlefield and shattered as a fighting force, while the nation of Kuwait was free from Saddam Hussein's domination, liberated with its government to be restored.

These, after all, were the primary objectives of the massive Coalition undertaking that had spanned seven months and led to the largest concentration of military manpower and hardware since World War Two. From the beginning, President Bush had made it clear to the Iraqi people that the world's gathering and armed response was to the aggression of Saddam Hussein.

"Let there be no misunderstanding," Bush said, in comments aimed directly at the Iraqi population on September 16, 1990, "we have no quarrel with the people of Iraq. I've said

President Bush delivers a radio address from the Oval Office in January 1991. *(George HW Bush Presidential Library and Museum via Wikimedia Commons)*

many times, and I will repeat right now, our only object is to oppose the invasion ordered by Saddam Hussein… Saddam Hussein has told you that Iraqi troops were invited into Kuwait. That's not true… Saddam Hussein tells you that this crisis is a struggle between Iraq and America. In fact, it is Iraq against the world…"

With the unleashing of the air and ground onslaught, the leaders of the Coalition were keenly aware that their objectives had to be achieved. However, in the event the absolute devastation of the Iraqi military, and the continuing hardships that were necessarily visited upon the Iraqi people,

Iraqi infrastructure was destroyed by heavy Coalition air and ground attacks, compelling Saddam Hussein to retreat from Kuwait. *(US Department of Defense via Wikimedia Commons)*

were cause for consideration. After lengthy air bombardment and 100 hours of ground combat, images of carnage and destruction were being broadcast around the world. Humanitarian concerns began to weigh heavily on further prosecution of the Gulf War. The horrific spectacle of charred bodies unburied in the desert sun along the so-called Highway of Death invited criticism.

After making the ceasefire announcement, President Bush asked Iraqi military commanders to meet with Coalition officers within 48 hours to arrange for the conclusion of hostilities and dispatched Secretary of State James Baker to the Middle East to frame the long-term basis for peace.

"Seven months ago, America and the world drew a line in the sand," Bush announced. "We declared that the aggression against Kuwait would not stand, and tonight America

Egyptian troops, along with those of other Middle Eastern nations, stand in ranks for review during Desert Storm. *(US Navy via Wikimedia Commons)*

An American soldier sits atop a BMP armoured personnel carrier of the Kuwaiti army after the Desert Storm ceasefire. *(US Navy via Wikimedia Commons)*

and the world have kept their word. This is not a time of euphoria, certainly not a time to gloat, but it is a time of pride."

Meanwhile, General Norman Schwarzkopf, commander of Coalition forces, praised the prowess of the multi-national force that won the victory. After the preparatory air campaign, ground forces led by the mighty armour of the US and British armies had crushed the Iraqi military and its vaunted Republican Guard. Schwarzkopf reported that at least 3,700 Iraqi tanks had been destroyed or captured, along with 2,140 enemy artillery pieces. An estimated 85,000 to 100,000 Iraqi soldiers were dead or wounded, while another 85,000 or more were currently prisoners of war. In sharp contrast, Coalition casualties were light, with estimates of 300 to 400 killed, and fewer than 1,000 wounded in both combat and non-combat circumstances.

On the same day that the ceasefire was declared, Iraqi representatives accepted 12 United Nations Security Council resolutions that initiated the peace process. The terms of the settlement were formalised within weeks and took effect on April 11, 1991. They included a formal Iraqi denunciation of international terrorism and a cessation of state sponsorship of such activities, the elimination of any and all Iraqi weapons of mass destruction, including chemical and biological ordnance, along with ballistic missiles of a certain range. Nuclear facilities were to be inspected by a special UN commission and the International Atomic Energy Agency. Prisoners and detainees were to be returned to their home countries, while a demilitarised zone, supervised by the UN, would be established along the Iraqi border with Kuwait. Iraq agreed to recognise and respect Kuwaiti sovereignty and to accept responsibility for damage caused, atoning with reparations payments.

Although the shooting war had ended, post-conflict analysis and criticism soon emerged. It seemed to many military and political observers around the world that unfinished business – in fact the seeds of future conflict – loomed. The odious Saddam Hussein remained in power, and he was not to be trusted. Saddam soon enough resumed his threats and warmongering, destabilising the region to the best of his ability. His government repeatedly stonewalled inspections of nuclear and other facilities in the country, and violated the terms of the peace.

The continuation of the Desert Storm fighting would no doubt have produced a heightened humanitarian crisis, but so did the ceasefire, which some deemed simply too lenient. With the benefit of historical hindsight, it might be easy to conclude that the end of the Gulf War left a despot in power in Iraq and spawned further atrocities against the Iraqi people, particularly the minorities that were long oppressed in the country. However, the aftermath of the 2003 Iraq War, which did topple Saddam Hussein, brought destabilisation, chaos, and death as well, while the United States and its allies struggled in the costly but futile exercise of nation building. ■

Iraqi Kurds, fearing vengeance from Saddam Hussein, flee towards the Turkish border in the wake of the Gulf War. *(US Department of Defense via Wikimedia Commons)*

HEROES OF DESERT STORM

The SA-13 *Gopher* surface-to-air missile presented an extreme hazard to low-flying Coalition aircraft. *(Public Domain One half 3544 via Wikimedia Commons)*

Shown with the rank of major general, then-Captain Paul T Johnson received the Air Force Cross during the Gulf War. *(US Government via Wikimedia Commons)*

THE MORNING MISSION of February 15, 1991, was straightforward for the two A-10 Warthog pilots of the 353rd Tactical Fighter Squadron, 354th Tactical Fighter Wing based at King Fahd International Airport in Saudi Arabia – strike an Iraqi refuelling tanker and then attack targets to the north.

Captain Stephen R Phillis and his wingman 1st Lieutenant Robert Sweet took to the air, blasted the tanker, and then teamed with F-16 Fighting Falcons in the vicinity of Basra, Iraq. Anti-aircraft fire was thick, including surface-to-air missiles (SAMs), so Phillis ordered a swing back towards the original target. Soon enough, elements of the Iraqi al-Medinah

Captain Paul Johnson rides in a 1991 parade with actress Brooke Shields. *(US National Archives and Records Administration via Wikimedia Commons)*

Division stretched out below them, tanks, armoured personnel carriers, infantry.

The two American pilots made firing passes at the enemy, flying relatively low and slow in a characteristic Warthog attack. In seconds, an Iraqi SA-13 missile site had fired at the A-10s. Sweet was struck by a SAM that heavily damaged his plane, and he ejected and came to earth close to enemy troops he had been bombing and strafing just moments earlier.

Phillis saw the imminent danger to his wingman. Rather than simply relaying the coordinates of the shootdown for search and rescue and then flying to safety, he chose to stay close to his friend and offer what protection he could. The pilot switched to Sandy, the A-10 search and rescue mode, and relayed the information to an AWACS plane aloft at some distance. As another flight of A-10s approached, he tried to direct them towards his position, firing flares to attract the attention of the incoming friendly aircraft and to divert the Iraqi ground fire in his own direction.

Wham! An SA-13 found its mark, and Phillis knew his aircraft had taken serious damage. He calmly radioed that his plane was going down. "Enfield 3-7 is bag as well," he alerted the AWACS. The A-10 was on fire, and Phillis turned south to distance himself from Sweet's location so that rescue personnel might get to the wingman first. His A-10 then lost power and careened into the ground. Phillis had died to save his

A-10 Warthog attack aircraft sits on the tarmac at King Fahd International Airport. *(US Air Force via Wikimedia Commons)*

wingman. Sweet was captured and held by the Iraqis for about three weeks before his release.

The courageous Phillis had given his life for his friend. He was awarded a posthumous Silver Star. However, a grass roots movement to upgrade the decoration to the Medal of Honor may be gaining traction, with retired Gulf War veteran and Florida Air National Guard General Jim Demarest leading the effort.

Other incidents of incredible bravery occurred throughout the seven months of Desert Shield/Storm. US Army, Air Force, Navy, and Marine Corps personnel exhibited incredible heroism and fortitude regularly, as did Coalition partner forces, including those of the British Army, Royal Air Force, Royal Marines, and Royal Navy.

US Air Force Captain Paul Johnson received the Air Force Cross for an hours-long mission on January 21, 1991, while carrying out orders to search for an F-14 Tomcat fighter crew that had been shot down the previous night. Johnson led his flight of A-10s through an attack on an Iraqi Scud missile site, three aerial refuelling procedures, and three hours of intense searching for the downed aircrew. When an Iraqi truck appeared, heading towards one of the survivors, Johnson's aircraft took it out, allowing the rescue to proceed.

Air Force Captain William F Andrews also received the Air Force Cross. He was shot down, sustained a broken leg, and was captured when his F-16 was struck by ground fire during an attack on an Iraqi mechanised column on February 27. After ejecting, Andrews endured great pain but stayed in contact with other pilots, warning them when SAMs were launched, and advising them to take evasive action. When the mission was completed, several of Andrews' comrades testified that his reports and timely alerts kept them from being shot down as well.

Among the recipients of the Navy Cross, Lieutenant Colonel Michael Kurth, US Marine

Royal Navy Commander Richard Jeffrey Ibbotson received the Distinguished Service Cross while in command of the mine countermeasures vessel HMS *Hurworth.* *(Government of the United Kingdom via Wikimedia Commons)*

First Lieutenant Kevin McElroy saved an EF-111 aircraft in the performance of his radar jamming duties. *(Creative Commons Thornfield Hall via Wikimedia Commons)*

These aircraft of the 7440th Composite Wing (Provisional) were based at Incirlik, Turkey, during the Gulf War. *(US Government via Wikimedia Commons)*

The wreckage of this F-16 Fighting Falcon strike aircraft was found in the desert by US Marines. *(US Government via Wikimedia Commons)*

Corps, stands out. On February 26, he led a Marine light helicopter squadron in daring fire support missions as ground troops fought the Iraqis near the burning Al Burgan oil fields. During ten hours of combat, visibility limited by the smoke and flames, Kurth commanded multiple strike flights that resulted in the destruction of at least 70 enemy armoured vehicles.

Captain Eddie Ray commanded Company B, 1st Light Armored Infantry Battalion, 1st Marine Division in Kuwait on February 21.

Wing Commander, and later Air Chief Marshal, Sir Glenn Torpy received the Distinguished Service Order for command of No 13 Squadron, RAF and Reconnaissance Element. *(US Air Force via Wikimedia Commons)*

As a component of Task Force Shepherd, the company was engaged in blunting an Iraqi armoured counterattack west of the Burgan oil fields. During ten hours of combat, Ray skilfully manoeuvred his company in co-ordination with Apache attack helicopters and TOW anti-tank missile teams against the numerically superior foe. When the fight was over, at least 50 Iraqi armoured personnel carriers had been destroyed and 250 enemy soldiers taken prisoner.

Army Sergeant Young M Dillon received a posthumous Silver Star for gallantry while serving with the Headquarters Battery, 82nd Field Artillery Battalion, 3rd Armored Division. He was among numerous recipients of the decoration, including Marine Corporal Bryan R Freeman of the 1st Tank Battalion, 1st Marine Division. Freeman and his scout team were busy marking a helicopter landing zone when an enemy mechanised brigade struck the area. Responding quickly, Freeman relocated his team to the left flank and immediately spotted three Iraqi tanks. He directed Hellfire missiles that blasted two of them and then turned to destroy a third. Spotting an Iraqi anti-aircraft position that was too distant for attack helicopters to take out, he sent four more Hellfire missiles hissing towards this target, and achieved three hits that silenced the enemy fire.

First Lieutenant Kevin McElroy of the Air Force flew as an electronic warfare officer with the 7440th Combat Wing out of Incirlik, Turkey, on February 18. While participating in the destruction of Iraqi airfields at Qayyarah South and Qayyarah West in northern Iraq, his EF-111 aircraft experienced a double engine compressor stall and lost power. Coolly, McElroy continued his vital work of jamming enemy surveillance equipment, while working with the pilot to restore thrust to one of the plane's engines, which regained function allowing the valuable aircraft to return safely to base. Meanwhile, McElroy's maintenance of the jamming effort allowed all 40 attack aircraft involved in the mission to also return safely.

Senior officers among the British contingent received the Distinguished Service Order for outstanding command. Among them were General Sir Rupert Smith, commander of the 1st Armoured Division, Wing Commander John Anthony Broadbent of No 15 Squadron, RAF, and Wing Commander Ian Travers Smith, leader of No 16 Squadron, RAF. The members of the ill-fated Bravo Two Zero SAS mission were awarded several medals.

Warrant Officer Class 1 Peter Ratcliffe, Warrant Officer Class 2 Stephen Francis Maguire, Staff Sergeant Kevin Michael Davies, Sergeant Steven Billy Mitchell, Sergeant Terence Powell, Corporal Floyd Matthew Woodrow, and unidentified members of the SAS and Special Boat Service received the Distinguished Conduct Medal, second only to the Victoria Cross, for heroism in the face of the enemy. ■

DESERT STORM TIMELINE

EVENTS MOVED SWIFTLY after the Iraqi occupation of Kuwait, and within seven months the Coalition military alliance had won the victory. Representatives of the Iraqi government formally accepted terms of surrender on March 3, 1991, and Coalition prisoners of war held in Iraq were released two days later.

1990

July

17 Saddam Hussein levels charges against Kuwait, asserting that his neighbour has engaged in overproduction of oil and illegally stolen oil from the reserves of the Rumaila oil field.

25 US Ambassador April Glaspie meets with Saddam Hussein and in controversial comments, infers that the dispute between Iraq and Kuwait is a matter for Arab countries to resolve.

August

2 Saddam Hussein orders Iraqi military forces to invade Kuwait. Responding immediately, President George HW Bush freezes Kuwaiti and Iraqi assets in the United States, and the United Nations calls for the immediate withdrawal of the Iraqi army. Bush also orders the aircraft carrier USS Independence strike group to the Persian Gulf.

6 The United Nations Security Council authorises the imposition of sweeping economic sanctions against Iraq in an effort to compel Saddam Hussein to withdraw from Kuwait.

7 President Bush initiates Operation Desert Shield, the organisation of a multi-national military force and the subsequent build-up of armed might that would oppose the aggression of Saddam Hussein against Kuwait. Secretary of Defense Dick Cheney visits Saudi Arabia, and a request for military aid is received from that government;

elements of the 82nd Airborne Division are activated for deployment along with Air Force fighter and attack squadrons.

8 In a gesture of defiance against growing pressure, Saddam Hussein annexes Kuwait as a province of Iraq and begins the installation of a puppet government. Most nations refuse to acknowledge the political move.

9 The United Nations repudiates the Iraqi annexation of Kuwait, declaring the action invalid.

12 The US government enacts a campaign of interdiction and blockade against Iraqi shipping.

22 President Bush begins the call-up of US military reserves in preparation for deployment to the Middle East.

September

9 President Bush and Soviet President Mikhail Gorbachev meet in Helsinki, Finland, and release a joint statement supporting United Nations resolutions.

14 Iraqi forces take control of numerous foreign missions in Kuwait City. The UK and France announce the deployment of troops to Saudi Arabia. By mid-October, nearly 230,000 troops are there, and 200,000 of them are American.

October

29 The United Nations demands that Iraqi forces discontinue the mistreatment of Kuwaiti civilians and foreign nationals, warning Saddam Hussein that his government is liable for damages caused.

Iraqi dictator Saddam Hussein sparked the Gulf War with the seizure of Kuwait. *(Iraqi News Agency via Wikimedia Commons)*

November

8 President Bush orders the military capability of the Desert Shield build-up to reach an offensive option rather than solely as a deterrent to further Iraqi expansion.

20 Forty-five members of the Democratic Party file suit to force President Bush to seek Congressional approval for further military action. The lawsuit is eventually dismissed.

22 President Bush and the First Lady visit troops in the Middle East for Thanksgiving dinner.

29 The United Nations Security Council votes to authorise the use of force if Iraq does not end its occupation of Kuwait by midnight of January 15, 1991.

President Bush meets with advisors during the 1990 Helsinki summit with Soviet leader Mikhail Gorbachev. *(George HW Bush Presidential Library via Wikimedia Commons)*

A US Navy F/A-18 Hornet fighter flies above the aircraft carrier USS *Saratoga* during Desert Shield. *(National Museum of the US Navy via Wikimedia Commons)*

French soldiers stand in ranks during a review, as operation Desert Shield builds.
(US Army via Wikimedia Commons)

30 Still attempting to resolve the crisis by diplomatic means, President Bush invites Iraqi Foreign Minister Tariq Aziz to Washington, DC, and offers to send Secretary of State James Baker to Baghdad.

1991

January

9 Secretary of State James Baker and Foreign Minister Tariq Aziz meet for six hours in Geneva, Switzerland, but no progress is made towards a peaceful resolution.

12 The US Congress approves the use of American military forces in offensive operations against Iraqi forces in the Persian Gulf region.

15 The United Nations deadline for Iraqi withdrawal passes with no action from Saddam Hussein.

17 At 3am local time, Operation Desert Storm begins with air attacks and the launching of cruise missiles against high value targets in Baghdad and across Iraq. Saddam Hussein announces that the "Mother of all Battles" has begun. Iraqi Scud missiles are launched against Israel.

18 Following extensive consultation with the government of Israel, President Bush announces that the Israeli military will not retaliate against Iraq for Scud missile launches.

19 The US deploys Patriot anti-missile missiles to defend Coalition countries in the region, as well as Israel, after three Iraqi Scud missiles hit the Israeli city of Tel Aviv. US forces seize Iraqi oil platforms in the Persian Gulf, capturing the first enemy prisoners of war.

20 Captured Coalition airmen, whose planes have been shot down, are paraded before cameras by Iraqi television in a propaganda move. Ten Iraqi Scud missiles are launched against Saudi Arabia, nine of them intercepted with one veering into the sea.

22 Iraqi soldiers set fire to Kuwaiti oil wells and reserve tanks, initiating an environmental disaster.

23 After striking a suspected Iraqi chemical weapons facility, US officials deny accusations that they have destroyed a baby formula factory.

24 Coalition air combat sorties surpass 15,000 during the ongoing campaign to degrade Iraqi capabilities to wage war.

26 USAF F-15 Eagle air superiority fighters shoot down three Iraqi MiG-23 fighters in one of the earliest air-to-air engagements of the Gulf War. The US government confirms the historic submarine launch of a Tomahawk cruise missile from USS *Louisville*.

29 The US and Soviet governments offer a ceasefire to Iraq in exchange for withdrawal from Kuwait. Iraqi soldiers have dumped millions of gallons of oil into the Persian Gulf. Iraqi forces invade Saudi Arabia, seizing the town of Khafji.

30 In the first ground battle of the Gulf War, Coalition forces, including US, Saudi, and Qatari units begin operations to retake Khafji.

31 Coalition forces defeat the Iraqis and reoccupy Khafji.

February

1 Coalition air forces devastate an Iraqi armoured column headed towards the Saudi frontier on a ten-mile stretch of open road.

4 The battleship USS *Missouri* fires its main 16in batteries in action for the first time since the Korean War.

6 USF-15 fighters shoot down four Iraqi aircraft during an attempt by Saddam Hussein's air force to flee to neighbouring Iran.

8 Secretary of Defense Dick Cheney travels to Saudi Arabia and raises the probability of a coming ground offensive.

13 US aircraft bomb an underground bunker believed to be a command-and-control centre causing numerous casualties, although Iraqi officials assert that it was a civilian air raid shelter.

14 The US military announces the severe degradation of Iraqi combat capability via the air campaign, with more than 4,000 tanks and armoured vehicles destroyed.

16 Abdul Amir al-Anbari, Iraqi Ambassador to the United Nations, threatens to use weapons of mass destruction if the Coalition air campaign is not suspended.

18 The helicopter assault carrier USS *Tripoli* and guided missile cruiser USS *Princeton* are damaged by mines in the Persian Gulf.

24 At 4am local time, the ground phase of Desert Storm begins. Casualties are light, and immediate Iraqi resistance is only sporadic as many soldiers capitulate at the sight of Coalition forces.

25 The rapid advance of Coalition ground forces is noted, with troops positioned to

A Coalition Vulcan self-propelled anti-aircraft weapon sits poised for the beginning of the Desert Storm ground war. *(US National Archives and Records Administration via Wikimedia Commons)*

An Israeli family dons gas masks and takes shelter amid the threat of Scud missile attack.
(Government Press Office (Israel) via Wikimedia Commons)

liberate Kuwait City. An estimated 25,000 Iraqi soldiers surrender to Coalition forces. An Iraqi Scud missile strikes a US barracks in Dhahran, killing 28 and wounding 98.

26   US armoured forces rout the Iraqis at the Battle of 73 Easting. Kuwaiti resistance forces announce that they control Kuwait

US soldiers survey the damage done to an Army barracks in Dhahran, Saudi Arabia, which killed 28 Americans. *(US Army via Wikimedia Commons)*

Kuwaiti civilians and Coalition soldiers celebrate the end of the Gulf War.
(US Department of Defense via Wikimedia Commons)

City. Retreating Iraqi troops and vehicles are ravaged along Highway 80 out of Kuwait towards Iraq; the route is soon to be referred to as the Highway of Death.

27   Iraqi forces are defeated at the Battle of Medina Ridge, while the Republican Guard is further pounded during the Battle of Norfolk. Coalition forces

seize Kuwait International Airport. Coalition officials announce that approximately half the Iraqi army has been destroyed and 100,000 of its troops have been taken prisoner.

28   President Bush announces a ceasefire and publishes conditions for permanent cessation of hostilities. ■

President George HW Bush greets General Norman Schwarzkopf during ceremonies honouring forces returning from the Gulf War.
(US National Archives and Records Administration)

DESERT STORM
IN FILM AND MEDIA

MODERN WARFARE ON land, sea, and air, as prosecuted during Operation Desert Storm 35 years ago brought an immediacy of the violence and destruction into public view like never before. The aftermath of the conflict further gave rise to glimpses of real fighting – from senior commanders to individual soldiers, sailors, and airmen who later recounted their stories.

In memoirs, interviews, real-time camera footage, investigative reports, and riveting recreations of incidents, the Gulf War has been remembered in the media. Veterans, historians, and political figures of the period have contributed to the body of work available for future generations to evaluate. They range from revelations of covert operations to the inspiring stories of personal bravery, the political wrangling and the leaders who shaped the course of the build-up, the unleashing of military might against the aggression of Saddam Hussein, and the struggles of post-traumatic stress disorder, and impact of Gulf War Syndrome on veterans' health.

Less than two years after the Gulf War ended, General Norman Schwarzkopf, commander of the multi-national Coalition military force that defeated the Iraqi armed forces, published the most prominent memoir of the Desert Storm period. Schwarzkopf became a national hero in the United States and a worldwide figure of adulation after the conflict. However, his frank assessment of the strain of command – sending men and women into harm's way – is clearly described.

Colin Armstrong, using the pen name of Chris Ryan, wrote his account of the Bravo Two Zero mission. *(Creative Commons James English via Wikimedia Commons)*

Author Anthony Swofford's controversial book *Jarhead*, was later turned into a film. *(Creative Commons Kellyjeanne9 via Wikimedia Commons)*

Sean Bean in *Bravo Two Zero*. *(BBC)*

Denzel Washington in *Courage Under Fire*. *(Fox 2000 Pictures)*

In his book *It Doesn't Take A Hero*, Schwarzkopf reflected of his time in the crucible of command: "It doesn't take a hero to order men into battle. It takes a hero to be one of those men who goes into battle. Any soldier worth his salt should be anti-war; and still there are things worth fighting for."

Four years after his service as a sniper with the 2nd Battalion, 7th Marines, in Desert

Samuel L Jackson in *Rules of Engagement*. *(Paramount Pictures)*

Storm ended, Anthony Swofford began writing his story. *Jarhead: A Marine's Chronicle of the Gulf War and Other Battles*, relates a journey of enlistment as a teenager through training, deployment, and combat experience. The book generated both positive and negative reviews and commentary; some hailing the work as a realistic perspective on a young Marine in wartime, and others as an overly critical discourse on life in the US Marine Corps. The book was the basis for the 2005 film *Jarhead* starring Jake Gyllenhaal, Jamie Fox, Peter Saarsgard, and Lucas Black.

General Peter de la Billière, deputy commander of Coalition forces, wrote a memoir titled *Storm Command: Personal Account of the Gulf War*, while author Jean Edward Smith wrote *George Bush's War*, and Dilip Hiro penned *Desert Shield to Desert Storm*.

Writing with the pen name Andy McNab, SAS veteran Steven Billy Mitchell wrote the book *Bravo Two Zero*, published in 1993, recounting the harrowing experience of an eight-man

Author Rick Atkinson wrote a definitive account of the Gulf War. *(Creative Commons Library of Congress Life via Wikimedia Commons)*

special operations mission behind Iraqi lines. Reflecting on the stress of combat, Mitchell wrote: "You've got to move forward and take the fight to them. It's the last thing they're expecting. You're dead anyway. So, anything you do is a bonus... They can break any bone in your body that they choose, but it's up to you whether or not they break your mind." A dramatised adaptation of the book starring Sean Bean was televised by the BBC in 1999.

Another member of the Bravo Two Zero SAS team, Colin Armstrong, wrote his version of the ordeal under the pen name Chris Ryan. *The One That Got Away*, published in 1995, presents contradictions to Mitchell's version of the mission gone awry, and elicited criticism from other surviving members of the mission. The resulting controversy spawned author Michael Asher's 2003 re-examination of the events in his investigative work titled *The Real Bravo Two Zero*, as well as a rebuttal publication titled *Soldier Five* by former team member Mike Coburn, with input from SAS team comrade Malcolm MacGown.

In 1996, the ITV television film *The One That Got Away* told the story of Bravo Two Zero from Armstrong's point of view. Three years later, a two-hour television mini-series was broadcast with the perspective of Mitchell driving the narrative.

Helena Bonham Carter and Michael Keaton in *Live From Baghdad*. *(HBO Films)*

Meg Ryan in *Courage Under Fire*. *(Fox 2000 Pictures)*

Stark Sands and Alexander Skarsgård in the TV adaptation *Generation Kill*. *(HBO)*

The poster for the 1999 satirical war movie *Three Kings*. *(Warner Bros)*

In 2004, journalist Evan Wright published the book *Generation Kill*, recounting his experiences while embedded for two months with the 1st Reconnaissance Battalion 'Devil Dogs' of the US Marine Corps during the push to Baghdad in 2003. The book was based on three articles he had written for *Rolling Stone* magazine, which won had won the National Magazine Award for Excellence in Reporting. It was later adapted as a seven-part TV series starring Alexander Skarsgård, James Ransone and Stark Sands.

Another notable firsthand account of the Gulf War is William L Smallwood's *Warthog: Flying the A-10 in the Gulf War* published in 1993. A second A-10 pilot, Buck Wyndham, wrote *Hogs in the Sand: A Gulf War A-10 Pilot's Combat Journal*, released in 2020.

Wyndham wrote of his experience: "I am awed by my destructive power. With a small squeeze of the gun trigger under my right index finger, I can rip the turret off a 30-ton battle tank and throw it 200ft across the desert, while the rest of the tank burns in an explosion of white-hot, burning phosphorescence. But the cold, morbid reality of it does not exist from where I sit and watch it happen. There's no dramatic chord. No deafening explosion. No screams suddenly stifled. The soundtrack of a pilot's war is mostly silent..."

Historical accounts of the Gulf War are led by acclaimed historian Rick Atkinson's *Crusade:*

The 1st Reconnaissance Battalion 'Devil Dogs' in the TV mini-series *Generation Kill*. (HBO)

Burning oilfields in *Jarhead*. (Universal Pictures)

Journalist Evan Wright's award-winning book *Generation Kill* was adapted for TV in 2008. (HBO)

The Untold Story of the Gulf War, released in 1994. In addition, *The Gulf War Chronicles: A Military History of the First War with Iraq* by Richard S. Lowery, published in 2008, presents an overview of Desert Storm and its modern technology implementation. Famed Watergate reporter Bob Woodward wrote *The Commanders*, and noted historian Walter J Boyne added *Gulf War: A Comprehensive Guide to People, Places & Weapons*.

Noteworthy books relating more specific aspects of Desert Storm include *Storm on the Horizon: Khafji – The Battle that Changed the Course of the Gulf War* by David J. Morris, *Desert Storm Air War: The Aerial Campaign Against Saddam's Iraq in the Gulf War* by Jim Corrigan, *Moving Mountains: Lessons in Leadership and Logistics* from the Gulf War by William Pagonis and Jeffrey Cruikshank, and *Warrior's Rage: The Great Tank Battle of 73 Easting* by Douglas MacGregor, a veteran of the US Army.

In the immediate aftermath of the Gulf War, various publishers rushed to place histories of Desert Shield and Desert Storm in retail outlets. These included *Time Magazine*, *National Geographic*, CNN, and other news and popular history outlets.

Feature films run the gamut from fact to fiction regarding Desert Storm. In *Live From Baghdad*, starring Michael Keaton, a CNN film crew led by Robert Wiener, whose book of the same name inspired the movie, works its way into Baghdad for timely coverage. *Three Kings* starring George Clooney, Mark Wahlberg, and Ice Cube, *The Finest Hour* starring Rob Lowe, *Courage Under Fire* starring Denzel Washington, Meg Ryan, and Lou Diamond Phillips, and *Rules of Engagement* with Tommy Lee Jones and Samuel L Jackson, tell fictional stories of bravery and controversy against the backdrop of Desert Storm, while *Thanks of a Grateful Nation* starring Ted Danson, Jennifer Jason Leigh, and Brian Dennehy explores medical issues experienced by veterans. Oscar-winning director Jonathan Demme, filmed an updated adaptation of the classic Cold War thriller *The Manchurian Candidate*, setting it against the backdrop of the Gulf War and starring Denzel Washington, Liev Schreiber, Jeffrey Wright, and Meryl Streep.

Documentaries surrounding Desert Storm include CNN's *Desert Storm: The War Begins*, the Apple TV series *Operation Desert Storm*, *The Hidden Wars of Desert Storm*, which was the result of a two-year research project examining documents and conducting interviews with major figures, *Battlezone: the Gulf War* also from Apple TV, *The Persian Gulf War* from the US Public Broadcasting System, and *After Desert Storm* from Al Jazeera, to name a few.

Video gamers have become immersed in the Gulf War with the 1991 release of *Operation: Desert Storm* from Bungie, and *Conflict: Desert Storm* and *Conflict: Desert Storm II* (2002; 2003) developed by Pivotal Games.

As Desert Storm passes further into history, no doubt a broader wealth of information will surface, allowing further in-depth exploration and analysis of the war that brought Saddam Hussein to his knees but left him in power for more than a decade. ■

Ice Cube, George Clooney and Spike Jonze in *Three Kings*. (Warner Bros)

Jake Gyllenhaal in *Jarhead*. (Universal Pictures)

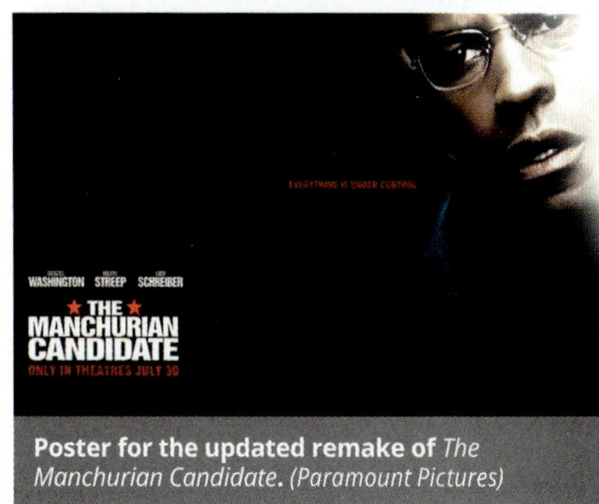

Poster for the updated remake of *The Manchurian Candidate*. (Paramount Pictures)

POSTSCRIPT

AT THE TIME of the Gulf War, HR McMaster was a junior officer, an armoured cavalryman whose command thoroughly defeated the enemy wherever it was encountered. He commented later: "There are two ways to fight the United States military: asymmetrically and stupid. Asymmetrically means you're going to try to avoid our strengths. In the 1991 Gulf War, it's like we called Saddam's army out into the schoolyard and beat up that army."

True enough, the strength of the US military was on full display during Operation Desert Shield/Storm. And the allied forces of the Coalition, principally those of the United Kingdom, demonstrated outstanding combat prowess.

However, through the lens of history, the real victory in war comes in winning the peace. The immediate priorities of the Coalition were achieved in the lightning prosecution of the war to liberate Kuwait from Iraqi oppression. Although there were tragic losses, the Coalition had prevailed in sweeping fashion and at minimal cost considering the projected casualties that were expected in the war. So, winning the peace became problematic for the rest of the world as Saddam Hussein held onto the government in Baghdad, and re-embarked on a campaign of genocide during the uprisings of the Shiite and Kurdish populations that followed his defeat in the Gulf War.

The Ba'athist strongman continued to arrest, imprison, and torture those who dissented. He remained defiant in the face of economic sanctions. He interfered with the inspections of nuclear and other facilities. He carried on the charade of a rebuilding military and the possibility of chemical and biological weapons being unleashed on his perceived "enemies", both foreign and at home.

What then, did the Coalition victory in the Gulf War 35 years ago accomplish? First, it demonstrated a global resolve

A British soldier provides security during a meeting of village leaders in northern Iraq and his superior officer, March 1991. *(US Department of Defense via Wikimedia Commons)*

General Colin Powell, Chairman of the US Joint Chiefs of Staff, and General Norman Schwarzkopf, commander of Coalition troops and his wife, Brenda, enjoy a victory parade. *(National Archives and Records Administration via Wikimedia Commons)*

to stand against armed aggression. Then, it became a proving ground for advancing technology in virtually every phase of military endeavour – the logistics triumph of Desert Shield was, in itself, a monumental achievement. Was the war just? Most would say yes. Was the victory complete? Many would say no.

In the end, amid so-called "evidence" that Iraq possessed weapons of mass destruction, the United States led another alliance, the Coalition of the Willing, to war in Iraq in 2003. Saddam was captured, tried, and found justice at the end of a rope. But American and Western involvement in Iraq during an agonising period of unrest dragged on for another eight years. ■

A Kuwaiti oil well set afire by Iraqi soldiers blazes in the waning hours of the Gulf War. *(US Army Corps of Engineers via Wikimedia Commons)*